T0323257

PRISONERS
OF THE
BRITISH

PRISONERS OF THE BRITISH

Internees and Prisoners of War During the First World War

MICHAEL FOLEY

FONTHILL

To lovely little Remee, a special little girl

Fonthill Media Language Policy

Fonthill Media publishes in the international English language market. One language edition is published worldwide. As there are minor differences in spelling and presentation, especially with regard to American English and British English, a policy is necessary to define which form of English to use. The Fonthill Policy is to use the form of English native to the author. Michael Foley was born, educated, and lives in London and therefore British English has been adopted in this publication.

Fonthill Media Limited
Fonthill Media LLC
www.fonthillmedia.com
office@fonthillmedia.com

First published in the United Kingdom and the United States of America 2015

British Library Cataloguing in Publication Data:
A catalogue record for this book is available from the British Library

Copyright © Michael Foley 2015

www.michael-foley-history-writer.co.uk

ISBN 978-1-78155-479-1

Typeset in 10.5pt on 13pt Sabon
Printed and bound by CPI Group (UK) Ltd, Croydon, CR0 4YY

CONTENTS

Introduction

One aspect often ignored in relation to the histories of the First World War is what happened to the prisoners that were taken by the Allies. This could often involve large numbers of men. In Britain, the press were quick to report on how British prisoners in Germany were treated or often mistreated. There was no doubt a high level of propaganda in relation to this from both sides. There were reports of German mistreatment of POWs, which often led to the poor treatment of German prisoners in Britain.

The bad treatment of POWs had a long history; in conflicts of the past it was not uncommon for enemy prisoners to be slaughtered, sold into slavery, or even maimed (such as blinding or removing hands) to prevent further action by them. The well-known two-fingered salute, reversed into a V for Victory by Churchill, supposedly originated as the sign of English longbow men to the French who would remove the fingers of captured bowmen to stop them using their weapons again.

It was during the Napoleonic wars that the treatment of prisoners began to show some improvement; in England special prisons were built for the captives, although the food the French prisoners were given in captivity in England would not be seen as very wholesome today. Weevil infested biscuits may sound less than appetizing, but the food they were given was often similar to what the British forces at the time ate as well. The Napoleonic period was also the first time that civilians were interned. This happened in both Britain and in France where those seen as enemy aliens were held captive, although this occurred in very small numbers. In Britain many Frenchmen were welcomed into the country, but these were escaping nobles from the fury of the mob and the guillotine. Even military prisoners of the period had a great deal of freedom; this was for the officers only, who were often granted parole and were free to wander around the towns they were based in. In many cases they became a part of the local society, when they mixed with those of a similar class to themselves.

During the Crimean War there were often reports of British soldiers being flogged as a punishment for minor crimes and yet there did not seem to be any evidence of Russian prisoners being mistreated in the same way. The Russian prisoners who were brought to Britain during the war were very well treated, and proved very popular with the British public. This was something that was later repeated when military prisoners in the First World War were better treated than civilian aliens.

In 1864, there was further improvement to the treatment of POWs after the Swiss government organised a conference in Geneva; from this conference came the first international agreement on the treatment of prisoners. How strictly this agreement was followed was debatable—even as late as the Second World War some nations mistreated their prisoners, both military and civilian.

The dawn of the twentieth century had on the whole led to moves towards more humane treatment of those taken in war. One of the first serious attempts to set international rules for the treatment of prisoners of war was the Hague Convention of 1907. This set out that each state involved in a war had to set up a bureau. The British Information Bureau was opened at 49 Wellington Street, London. These bureaus had three responsibilities:

1. To reply to all inquiries concerning prisoners, giving the names of any who had escaped.
2. To give a list of all prisoners' names, numbers, ranks, units, and whether they were injured, and the place of capture and the camp they were held in.
3. To collect from the field of battle and keep the personal effects of those that had died.

When the war began in 1914, Britain was a very different place compared to what it was today. Despite what has been written about the First World War being a modern war, the country was still quite backward outside of large cities. In many rural areas the population rarely left their towns or villages and in the more remote areas news of what was going on in the world was seldom known. For the majority of the young men who rushed to join the Army it was the first time they had left their local area; very few of them would have ever been to another country. It was during these years that the rural population were quick to suggest anti-German action, viewing the people of Germany almost as a different species. Strangely, it was the urban population (who were more familiar with foreigners) that took this view to heart. Of course, there was less chance of those in rural areas coming across a foreigner.

On the whole, the German military prisoners of war brought back to Britain were treated very well. This is not to say that there were never cases of mistreatment. There were a number of large camps set up all over the country for prisoners of war, often guarded by members of the military who were unfit to take part in the conflict in Europe.

As well as military POWs there were others who were interned in camps. These were those seen as enemy aliens. They were often people who had lived in Britain for many years, some even had children fighting for Britain, but they were still interned. At first the government refused to take action over the majority of those seen as enemy aliens; eventually, due to outbreaks of rioting and violence towards anyone with a foreign sounding name, they were forced to act. This was partly caused by a very anti-German press.

The violent events in relation to enemy aliens in times of conflict was not a new phenomenon. After the Great Fire of London in 1666, Dutchmen were attacked in the streets as suspects of starting the fires. This may have been understandable as Britain was at war with the Dutch at the time. However, Frenchmen and other foreigners were also attacked—some were hung by members of the public.

Government forces did try and protect these foreigners; the Duke of York was out on the streets fighting the flames, while his guards patrolled the streets and rescued a number of foreign victims of the mob. In the First World War the government did attempt to protect aliens subjected to violence, but were mainly unsuccessful. Public opinion and the views of the government were not always in tune.

The widespread internment of enemy aliens in the First World War was seen by many as an overreaction. While it did occur again during the Second World War, it was only for a year. During the First World War it last the entirety of the conflict and, in many cases, well beyond. The regulations that applied to military prisoners of war did not apply to civilians.

Whether the victims of the war were captured military men or those who had decided to settle in Britain before the war, the treatment and containment of these men makes an interesting history. Another aspect of these events, apart from the imprisonment of men, was how in many cases their families were left destitute.

The so-called enemy aliens who had been living in the country (in some cases for many years) were less popular than the German military prisoners who were brought back to Britain from the battlefields of Europe to be held in large camps. The German soldiers were often handed gifts of fruit and cigarettes by the public as they made their way to their camps. Meanwhile, civilians with German or even foreign sounding names were being attacked and looted—frequently called baby killers as they marched to their camps.

It had been some years since anyone in the country had seen prisoners of war brought to England. Only the very elderly in 1914 would have any memory of the Russians in the middle of the previous century. The German soldiers were probably seen as a novelty, while those of German origin living in the country were seen as traitors or even spies.

What does come as a surprise was the size of the problem. There were less than twenty camps for both military and civilian prisoners in Britain in late 1914. By the end of the war there were more than 500. Some were small workers camps and some hospitals were also classed as camps, but it is an incredibly high number, especially when one considers how it has been mainly ignored since then.

1

1914

Although there had been a number of conflicts involving Britain in the century before the First World War began, they had been distant events. The major conflicts being in the Crimea and, more recently, in South Africa. The last conflict involving Britain and a threat of invasion had been the Napoleonic Wars; these had ended almost a century before the First World War began.

The First World War had one major difference to the previous modern conflicts that Britain had fought. The fighting of previous conflicts had always taken place abroad and British civilians had not been in the firing line. That was to change with the use of airships and aircraft; once air raids and the shelling from German ships on coastal towns began it was civilians who were being injured and dying, not just the soldiers and sailors in some distant land. Another big difference with this conflict was the number of people from the countries that Britain was fighting who were living in the country. Why were there so many Germans in Britain at the outbreak of war? It was a question that can only be answered by going far back into history.

There had been Germans coming to Britain since the Middle Ages, but the numbers began to increase significantly during the nineteenth century. There does not seem to be any one reason for their arrival, although the political situation in Germany is often given as the main reason. It was partly due to a large growth in the German population, which seems to have been a greater reason than any form of political persecution.

In many rural settings land was often left to the oldest son, leaving the rest of the family with nothing. Many Germans saw their future as lying in more industrial countries such as America. The biggest peaks of German emigration were in 1864–73 and 1880–93, which coincided with booms in the American economy. Travelling from Europe to America in the nineteenth century usually meant a stopover in Britain before a ship crossed the Atlantic. In some cases the German travellers arrived in Britain and went no further. There may have been various reasons for this, some may have run out of money and others may have got a job and decided to stay. Many German waiters came to Britain to improve their language, which gave them a better chance of a job back home. There was also the fact that Britain, like America, was more advanced economically than Germany or any other European country in the nineteenth century. There was a surplus population in Britain as well; while many immigrants may have arrived, many of the British population were also making their way across the Atlantic, especially from Ireland.

Although not the main reason for German emigration to Britain, there were increases in movement after three periods of political unrest or repression in Germany. These were in the 1830s, after 1848, and after 1850. It was not only politics that caused people to leave, after the unification of Germany, Bismarck passed a number of laws against Roman Catholics. Many schools and other organisations run by Catholics were closed and large numbers left the country, including many nuns. The situation for Roman Catholics may not have been much better in Britain at times in the nineteenth century, but in political terms the population of Britain was much freer than those in the rest of Europe. The country also had a policy of accepting anyone who wanted to come here. Whatever their reasons for coming here, until 1891 Germans were the largest foreign-born group in Britain and the majority of them lived in London. The Germans in Britain were one of the largest groups of immigrants and were only surpassed by the Irish and the Jews. Despite the number of immigrants in the country, the population of Britain was essentially an island race that had little to do with foreigners and had no idea of what other races were like. Perhaps this was what made them so susceptible to the belief that all aliens were treacherous and would betray them.

When war did start there were a large number of Germans in the country, many who had been here for years. Despite the fact that we were at war with Germany, *The Times* published advertisements from the German and Austrian embassies asking for their nationals to return home and enlist in the Army. Many young men left for

Germany before a system of permits was introduced to allow enemy aliens to leave the country. The outbreak of war led to an upsurge of patriotism in Britain; the newspapers were full of photographs of army units marching through the streets of England's cities. *War Illustrated* published a photograph of the Scots Guards marching through London with a small boy carrying the hat of his father in uniform, while the man carried a small girl on his shoulders. The same issue showed the Grenadier Guards on their way to Waterloo Station, with their wives walking alongside them—one with a child in a pushchair. The images showed how everyone supported and were excited about the war, even wives and children who seemed happy to see their men go off to fight.

The newspapers of the time have always portrayed this idea that everyone in the country was in favour of the war and that the majority of men could not wait to enlist. There is no doubt that this was true in many cases, but not everyone was so happy about the outbreak of war. Rudolf Rocker was a German immigrant who had lived in England for many years. He was a leading anarchist and had a great involvement in Jewish trade unions and worker movements before the war. His view of the reactions to war were very different to the one portrayed in the popular press. Rocker described the feeling of the threat of war as an ominous perception hanging over London. He said that the Labour Party were against the war and the liberal press favoured British neutrality. He also claimed that there was a powerful peace movement in the country. This is a fact rarely mentioned in most histories of the war. Rocker's view may have had something to do with his German origin, but there was some basis for his outlook.

On 2 August there was a large anti-war demonstration in Trafalgar Square, called by the Independent Labour Party. Rocker said that small noisy groups tried to break up the meeting, but they were unsuccessful. Rocker also described how when war was declared silent crowds watched the soldiers march off, they were not cheering and happy. It is interesting to look at the conflicting newspaper reports of the Trafalgar Square demonstration of 2 August. *The Times* claimed that many of those present were foreigners—mainly Germans. The report also said that at least a third of the crowd were supporters of the war and their singing of 'God Save the King' completely drowned out the socialist speakers, who could not be heard by those more than a few yards from their platform. *The Manchester Guardian* report gave a quite different view; they claimed that there was a large demonstration by socialists and that the crowds overflowed Trafalgar Square and stretched into the Strand and Whitehall. They claimed that the protesters were a few youths on the fringe of the crowd who waved Union Jacks, but were unsuccessful in causing any disruption.

Whether there was support for the war or not, one thing that did grip the country was the threat of invasion. The only reminders of the threat of foreign troops landing on our shores were some rarely used Martello Towers on the south and east coast, which had been built to deter Napoleon's troops from crossing the channel. The renewed threat of invasion was something no one alive had faced before. This led to a new panic over spies, who would be reporting back on the defences that existed to stop a German Army landing on our beaches. They had little to report on, the defences hardly existed and this did not seem to enter anyone's minds. Though it was no surprise that suspicion of spying should fall on those of enemy nationality already living in the country.

The spy scares may have been vastly exaggerated; however, according to the writer Tighe Hopkins, Germany had been sending spies into all other countries in Europe and to America for some time before the war even began. He did not distinguish between spies and saboteurs and he claimed that there were hundreds of men in the pay of Berlin working in France. He maintained that there were 1,600 foreigners and that these were educated and intelligent men who were employed on the French railways. The government demanded that all of these men became naturalised French citizens—182 refused and returned to Germany. Hopkins claimed that large numbers of German spies had also been operating in America long before they entered the war. There were plans to sabotage factories, encourage disruption through labour problems, and even attempt to bring America and Mexico to a state of war—this was towards a power with which Germany were still on friendly terms.

Strangely, considering his views, Hopkins claimed that there was no large system of spies operating in Britain. He did go on to allege that every German in the country should be seen as a possible spy, even someone such as a German barber may have been sending messages home. What important information a barber could have found that was useful to the German government was not explained. Hopkins' view no doubt mirrored that of many of the country's population in the early years of the war. The information that German civilians in Britain may have sent to Germany would only have been of low grade, which presented no danger.

Hopkins claimed that the German Army had a huge collection of disguises and that they had used men disguised as priests in Belgium; they had also been found in Australian uniforms in France. Despite his previous claim that men working as spies on the French railways were intelligent, educated persons he went on to claim that spies came from mongrel types, or were social pariahs who had no characters to lose.

It is interesting to read in one of the articles that Hopkins wrote for the *War Illustrated* that 'through postal censorship organised on military lines, it would be as easy at present to get a cipher message to the planet Jupiter as it would to Germany'. Hopkins died before the memoirs of Julius Crawford Silber were published, so he would not have seen how hollow his claims were. There were no doubt spies operating in Britain during the war. Julius Crawford Silber was of German descent and had worked as an interpreter for the British during the Boer War. He was in America when the war began and returned to Britain to work as a censor on military letters; he was eventually promoted to chief censor. After the war, he published his life story and admitted to being a German spy.

When the British tanks made their first appearance on the Somme, there was a belief that the Germans already knew about (what was supposed to be) one of their best kept secrets of the war. Silber had read a letter discussing the new weapon from a man at the tank headquarters at Eleveden to his wife; he had passed the information on to the Germans.

There had been rumours of German spies operating in the country for years before the war. A book published in 1909 by William Le Quex, entitled *Spies of the Kaiser*, was serialised in the press, so many must have suspected that spying was already occurring. In the early months of the war a number of men were executed for spying in France. The spy panic led to the challenging, or even the arrest, of anyone who was seen as acting suspiciously. This was especially true if the person acting suspiciously was of foreign descent. Guards were placed on bridges railway lines and even telegraph wires in case of espionage. It was debatable as to how widespread the presence of a German spy network was in the country. What was evident was that large numbers of Germans had been in Britain since the previous century; in 1914 there were close to 60,000 Germans in the country. Many of these had been in Britain for many years and had children and even grandchildren who were born here and saw themselves as British. Suspecting all of these people of being spies was of course ridiculous.

There would seem to have been some level of espionage taking place and one such event was reported on a troopship taking British soldiers to Boulogne in September. One of the ship's officers saw a man from the deck crew searching a dispatch box. He gave chase, but as the man left the ship two men appeared and one of them shot the ship's officer. There were even reports of British soldiers being arrested as spies. Two members of the Hampshire Regiment, a private and a lance corporal stationed at Codford in Surrey, were arrested with copies of letters regarding troop movements. It was reported that they had been proved to be spies.

There was an outbreak of rumours about the actions of enemy aliens living in Britain. This was reinforced with anti-German stories in the press, especially in the *Daily Mail*. This came as no surprise as the newspaper's owner, Lord Northcliffe, had been warning the public about Germany for years. The *Daily Mail* called on the public to refuse to be served by German waiters. However, the claims in sections of the press and from some right-wing politicians did have a great deal of influence on sections of the population.

Rudolf Rocker described the anti-alien newspapers as the yellow press. These included the daily newspapers such as the *Daily Mail*, the *Daily Express*, and the *Evening News* and weekly publications such as *John Bull*. The stories they published included German bakers putting arsenic in their bread, poisoning reservoirs that supplied London with drinking water, and even finding stocks of weapons in a German club. Rocker claimed that it was all ridiculous that the Germans living in England, many of whom had fled Germany's anti-socialist laws, should now be supporting the Kaiser.

The influence of the press was partly due to the increase in literacy among the general population. The majority of the working class did not have the enough experience of this new skill to be subjective about what they read, tending to believe everything that they saw written in the newspapers. The *John Bull* newspaper was one that was aimed at igniting the feeling of hatred against enemy aliens. It was owned by the politician Horatio Bottomley, who would also attract thousands of speakers to anti-Germen rallies at venues such as Trafalgar Square, as well as selling up to 2 million copies of his newspaper. Some of the rumours that began to circulate were little short of ridiculous. One was that a German Barber had threatened to cut the throat of any English customer that entered his shop. There was a strange conflict of attitude towards Germans by the British public. There had been a view that the British and the Germans had similar racial origins. This view was held by many, including a number of writers such as Thomas Carlyle and George Elliot. During the Victorian period many saw German education as a good role for Britain.

This was not completely followed by all and there were some anti-German demonstrations in the east end of London during the nineteenth century. This may have been partly due to a feeling against all immigrants at the time. Perhaps the best example of the anti-German feeling was the unpopularity of Prince Albert after he married Queen Victoria. The victory of the Prussians against France in 1870 was also a turning point in changing attitudes towards Germany, followed by their support for the Boers in the South African War.

A feeling of rivalry between Germany and Britain became the new opinion, with moves to restrict immigration into the country from 1905's Alien's Act. At the outbreak of war, a feeling of suspicion and fear had already taken root against the German population, with the British open to further persuasion and to the idea of internment. The government were in an unusual position at the start of the war, for much of it they seemed to be arguing against wholesale internment of enemy aliens and yet they had set up the Secret War Propaganda Bureau in 1914—this was run by Charles Masterman. The bureau produced pamphlets written by many of the best known writers of the time, which often promoted British patriotism by giving the impression that the Germans were a race that were to be hated. This no doubt helped to turn the population against enemy aliens and encouraged the idea of internment, which the government supposedly did not want. One reaction to this volatile situation was the formation of the Special Constabulary. Many police officers had left to join the Army and numbers were low. There was an upsurge of enthusiasm in joining this organisation. The Special Constabulary had not been used since the Chartist riots when they had only lasted a week. Soon men wearing armbands and carrying a baton and a whistle were the ones guarding bridges, telegraph wires, and important industrial sites against enemy aliens.

The level of anti-German feeling that was portrayed in the press was mainly reinforced amongst those of the lower classes. Much of the aristocracy, the upper classes, and the Royal Family had strong German connections. Robert Graves wrote that that when he joined the Army, four out of the five officers in his mess had German mothers or German fathers who were naturalised British subjects. One of

Graves's fellow officers told him that if he had not joined up when he did, he would have been accused of being a German spy. Another of the officers had an uncle interned in Alexandra Palace. Graves himself had four or five uncles in the opposite trenches; one of his uncles was a general in the German Army, while another was a British Admiral.

The outbreak of war was to have immediate effects on Germans in Britain—the August Bank Holiday was extended for banks, which did not open all week. The Stock Exchange closed, which turned out to be for much longer than had been planned; it did not reopen until January 1915. Gold coinage was retained by the banks and replaced with paper money.

The effect on the male population was enormous, with crowds besieging recruiting offices to go and do their bit by joining Kitchener's New Army. Many saw the war as an opportunity to escape their boring lives and have an adventure; it was also a chance to go abroad and see other countries. Few seemed to have any idea of what they would actually face during the fighting. The problem was what to do with the large number of recruits. There was a lack of accommodation, uniforms, and weapons; it was not unusual to see new army units drilling in public parks in civilian clothes with no weapons. Some recruits were sent home until they could be found somewhere to live.

When the Defence of the Realm Act was passed on 8 August it took away the rights of the population that had been experienced by them for years. Unsurprisingly a new opinion emerged—if the rights of the British citizens were to be removed, then so too should those of the foreigners in the country, to an even greater extent. When war broke out in August 1914 there were no immediate plans in place in Britain to intern foreign nationals; this was partly because the internment of civilians was not a normal practice of war, although it had happened at times in the past, on a very small scale in Britain during the Napoleonic Wars, in France under Napoleon, and in larger numbers in South Africa during the Boer War. Early on there were moves towards the detention of suspicious foreigners; on 5 August, Mr Reginald McKenna MP for Monmouth North asked to introduce a bill in Parliament to enable his majesty to impose restrictions on aliens, in times of war or national emergency. This was due to a number of cases of espionage being committed in recent years, according to Mr McKenna. He went on to claim that twenty-one spies had been arrested in the previous twenty-four hours. One of the first things to happen was the seizing of German ships in British ports. This included those in the London docks and two ships were seized in the Royal Victoria Dock. The crews, and in some cases the passengers, were taken off and interned.

Although the serious outbreaks of violence against foreign nationals occurred much later in the war, there were still a number of isolated incidents as soon as war was declared. Two men in Hull, Victor Parker and Joseph Connell, broke the window of a shop owned by a German. The magistrate in charge of their trial set a low tone for those responsible for maintaining the law, declaring that the men had just been displaying high spirits on their way to enlist—he fined them.

There were several panics about spies, but the Special Intelligence Department (founded in 1911) had been watching those suspected of being German spies for some time before the war—this was not public knowledge. Six suspected men were arrested and imprisoned before the war began, while others were kept under strict observation. Twenty more were arrested when war broke out and another 200, who had been under observation, were interned. *The Manchester Guardian* of 11 August reported on how many Germans had been arrested and their location. The report showed the variety of buildings used to house the early internees. According to the report, 200 had been taken to Olympia and were being guarded by British troops. Some of these were thought to be German reservists who were trying to leave the country and return to Germany. Others were there for not complying with the order to register.

At Swansea eighty-five aliens had been arrested and were under guard at Rutland Street School, waiting for a camp to be prepared. Fifty German seamen from captured ships were being held at Leith in Redford barracks and 120 Germans, mainly seamen and reservists, landed at Gosport harbour—they were marched away looking cheerful.

In Leeds a large number of Germans had been arrested, but only twelve were held and they were confined in the town hall. A disused engineering works on the banks of the River Dee (between Sandycroft and Queensferry near Chester) had been taken over as a place of detention. There were already 300 being held there that were guarded by the Chester territorials. These were mainly men who had been living in the area, but who had no one to vouch for them.

Many of those arrested had been held at the Olympia Exhibition Centre in London. A report in *The Times* on 14 August reported on the results of the spy fears; the report stated that the majority of them had been able to explain themselves and had later been released. Those that were still confined at the exhibition centre were mainly German sailors from ships detained in British ports. They were said to be very comfortable, despite the heat inside the centre due to the glass and steel construction of the building. They spent their time playing cards, reading *The Times*, or sleeping; they were also allowed visitors. As well as those held at Olympia, arrests were being carried out in other parts of the mainland and also in Dublin where 100 Germans had been arrested. Another 100 Germans were landed at Fort George, Inverness, who had been taken from trawlers in the North Sea. Despite the arrests, it was still possible for German, Austrian, and Hungarian subjects to apply for British naturalisation.

There seemed to be no clear rules as to who was to be arrested in the first months of the war. The camp that had been opened near Chester was quickly filling up; just over a week after *The Manchester Guardian* had reported that 300 Germans were held there, the number had risen to more than a 1,000. It was not described as a camp, but as a place of internment or an extemporised prison. The building was an old foundry that had been empty for some years. It was visible from trains on the Chester to Rhyl railway and there had been for some time a large for sale sign on what the newspaper described as a striking building. It resembled a fortification and it was surrounded with barbed wire fences.

The prisoners arrived by train in batches of forty to fifty under military guard. According to locals many of the men are of a good position and they seemed quite happy. There were also forty seamen arrested at Salford docks and three men in naval officer's uniform had been spotted who seemed to have access to parts of the camp that others did not. Singing and music is often heard to come from the buildings.

There was no real pressure on the government to intern all foreigners from enemy countries early in the war; whether this would have been possible is debatable. There was a severe shortage of accommodation for recruits to the Army, so finding accommodation for so many foreigners would have been impossible. There was also a serious problem with finding homes for the number of Belgian refugees arriving in the country who also had to be housed. A committee was formed to examine the problem of providing Civilian Internment Camps. This originally consisted of Sir William Byrne as chairman and Mr Sebag Montefiore as secretary. The two men went to the Isle of Man to establish whether a camp could be set up immediately for those who were being held in temporary accommodation in London and elsewhere. The holiday camp at Douglas was the obvious choice and barbed wire fences were erected around the site after it was taken over by the government. Buildings were added and gas and electricity was connected to the camp, but the early prisoners slept in tents. The first prisoners arrived in late September and Colonel Madoc was appointed as commandant.

The greatest number of complaints over the conditions of those interned seem to date from the early days of the process beginning. This was not due to mistreatment as such, but to the conditions that the newly interned men had to live in. In many cases accommodation for those guarding the internees were just as basic; many of the early camps were set up in places that were entirely unsuitable for people to live in. The same thing could have been said of early recruits to the Army. With the war beginning in the summer, recruits living in tents was more acceptable, but when they were still living under canvas during the winter, it caused an uprising of complaints for both the new recruits and the POWs and internees.

There was still no clear system of who was to be interned and at this time it was still mainly suspicious aliens or seamen from German ships. The problem that many of the Germans in Britain had was that when the war began they could not leave; this had only been possible for a few days. Paul Cohen-Portheim was a German artist who often visited England and when the war began he only had £10 and the banks were shut, so he could get no more money. Enemy aliens were in fact allowed to leave the country until the 10 August, but only from a number of selected ports. After this date they could only enter or leave with a special permit. Some aliens were allowed to go to America, but this was stopped before Cohen-Portheim could get a place. Again, any aliens entering the country were only allowed to land at the same ports that they could leave by. Many of the aliens in the country who were not interned were losing their jobs. It became very difficult for any alien to get work, which meant that even those who had not been interned could find themselves destitute.

Although there was some early hostility towards those who were seen as enemy aliens, this did not come from all areas. The Society of Friends (the Quakers) formed their own committee to help alien enemies rendered destitute by the war. They launched an appeal to raise money to do this within days of the war starting and this had the cooperation of the Home Office. The appeal raised nearly £6,000 within months of its conception—clearly not everyone was anti-German at this point. There were discrepancies in where support for the interned men's families came from. Both the British and German governments did at first support their own nationals living in the others country. The greater number of Germans in Britain made this an unbalanced expense for the British Government. Then Germany refused to pay for the British wives of German citizens in Britain, so the British Government retaliated. Germany later refused to pay for Germans whose sons were serving in the British Army, then for anyone who had lived in Britain for over ten years.

The society also played a role in making sure that the law was followed. Many of the aliens that approached them spoke no English and had been in hiding since the war began. Due to this they had no idea that they should have registered with the police. This was insisted on by the society before they would offer any help. The money was badly needed, as the society were besieged by hundreds of discharged German waiters. Many had lost their homes as well their employment. The majority had references from the best London hotels, but were sleeping in the capital's parks—a soup kitchen was opened for the men. The Friends Relief Society for Enemy Aliens recorded other cases of Germans becoming trapped in England. A German newspaperman, who was married to an English women, had arrived in the country to visit the wife's family, leaving their three young children with servants back in Germany. They were then stranded by the war and had to leave the wife's family home, as it was in a restricted area.

In another case, a German baron of poor health visited Britain and was arrested when war broke out. He had visited Olympia a few weeks earlier and seen monkeys in a cage; now he was sleeping in the same cage. He was eventually released and was housed in a German hotel by the society. Refused permission to return to Germany, he was again arrested during a police raid on the hotel. After a night in police cells he had a fit and was sent to an asylum where he died a few days later; it seems that he was mistaken for someone else of a similar name.

At times the situation that aliens found themselves in seemed like a hideous joke. One elderly man with an elderly wife had a strong German accent, but had lived in the country since he was a boy. He had brought up his own family and three orphaned grandchildren and when war broke out he and his wife were living with one of their children in Cardiff. The police forced them to move as Cardiff was a restricted area. When he approached the society for help they found that he was born in Heligoland when it was British. This meant that he was not actually an alien so they could not help him. However, he was too German for any British charity to help him. No German charity would help him because he was British. Eventually a private charity helped him.

The society had to be very careful that they were not seen to be disloyal in helping those seen as enemy aliens. The fact that many of the men working for the society were pacifists also put them in a position where they could be seen as unsupportive of the war effort. A number of the male members later served prison sentences for refusing to fight when conscription began. The society office was often the scene of those with a more patriotic turn of mind arriving and abusing them. There were often threats written on parcels delivered to the office or anonymous letters were sent containing threats. One letter contained threats to shoot the society secretary. This came as a shock to some members of the society, but what came as more of a shock were the attempts to persuade the British citizen that all Germans were fiends. This was seen as a means of persuading the nation that the removal of the citizens' rights and later conscription were necessary. Braithwaite in the report of the societies war work said that she had always thought that England was superior to such doings.

There were many new aliens arriving in the country, mainly from Belgium. Many of those arriving were penniless and had brought no more than they could carry with them and had to be found somewhere to live. The number of Belgians was to reach more than 200,000, although this tailed off by mid-1915. Finding homes for the new arrivals and large camps for interned aliens would have been a severe strain on the countries resources.

In September, the Alexandra Palace, which had until the war began been the sight of a cinema, roller skating rink, concert hall, monkey house, and a boating lake in the grounds, was taken over by the Metropolitan Asylum Board. The palace had closed to the public after war was declared. The board also took over Earls Court Exhibition Centre.

The board were to pay £250 per week for the palace, which included £20 worth of coal and the use of the palace catering staff. Within days 1,000 beds had been installed in the building and this rose to 3,000 soon after. There were 500 Belgian refugees living in the palace within a few weeks. These were then moved on to permanent homes and new arrivals took their place. The same process took place at Earls Court where there were 400 Belgian refugees living there within a few days and nearly 2,000 in the first week.

There was obviously a lot of disagreement over the facts of incidents of early conflict and the taking of military prisoners. During the naval action at Heligoland at the end of August it was claimed that German officers aboard the ships that were sunk by the British fired on their own men who had jumped overboard. This was denied by the German government who accused the British of firing on the men in the sea. The Germans also claimed that a British sailor had thrown a shell into a lifeboat full of German wounded. The British claimed that while German ships were sinking they had ceased fire to enable them to pick up survivors. Then one of the damaged German ships had again opened fire so they had to deal with this by again firing on the stricken ship. After this, while taking wounded Germen sailors on board, they again came under fire from a German cruiser. British sailors who were in a lifeboat with German wounded were removed, leaving the enemy in the boat. It was admitted that a British sailor on one of the British ships, angered at the actions of the German cruiser, did throw a shell into the lifeboat, but it did not explode. While admitting that this should not have happened, the British officers present repeated their claims that German officers did fire on their own men.

There were some German military prisoners being taken in the early part of the war, although it seems that the details for their care were still being finalised. It was decided in early September that captured officers would not receive full pay while in captivity, but be given advances for their needs, not exceeding half the pay of similar ranks in the British Army. Towards the end of September, reports on captured German military prisoners were appearing in the national press. *The Times* of 24 September published a story entitled 'Disillusioned Captives'; they claimed that the Germans had not been happy about fighting the war.

The *War Illustrated* published the story of five German soldiers who surrendered to two unarmed British motor bus drivers. The men were starving and happy to surrender. The report mentioned how, before Agincourt, Henry V told his officers that men who had no stomach for a fight should be sent away. The obvious insinuation was that this was the case with the enemy.

The first prisoners from the Battle of the Aisne arrived at Camberley and were described as well-built men who cheerfully marched 2 miles from the station to Frith Hill camp. Over a week, between 1,500 and

2,000 men arrived at the camp from the battle. Many of them spoke English and were allowed to speak to locals as they made their way to the camp. They were given gifts of cigarettes and fruit by local people. It seems that there was little antagonism against the military enemy at this early stage of the war. According to the report, many of the prisoners had not known that they were going to fight against Britain. Some claimed that they had been told that they would be fighting alongside the British against the French who had invaded Belgium. It was only after they were captured that they found out who they were fighting and why.

The early arrival of German military prisoners seemed to have aroused a lot of interest amongst the public and *The Times* published a number of stories about them. On 29 September they reported how German prisoners at Frimley were having a placid existence and seemed contented in their camp, despite being bored. Boredom was relieved by games of football and concerts by those with musical skills. Although the prisoners had money and could buy items from outside the camp, newspapers containing war news were banned. Some of the press had a more slanted emphasis to their stories. The *War Illustrated* asked if the kindness shown to prisoners of war in Britain was misguided; their lives were described as one of ease and enjoyment spent playing cards and leap frog. This was while British prisoners in Germany were forced to perform hard labour. The report also pointed out that while Kitchener's army was short of blankets the Germans in camps were given extra. There were already attempts to portray our men as suffering at the hands of the Germans in captivity, while the prisoners in Britain were having an easy time. There seemed to be an attempt to shame those members of the public who had handed out gifts to the arriving prisoners.

The arrival of a large group of Belgian refugees in Deptford in October was to have an immediate effect on the area. The stories of German atrocities were already well known, but the sight of these people, who had to leave their homes to escape the Germans, seemed to inspire locals and rioting broke out in the area. This spread to nearby areas such as Brixton and Catford.

There seemed to be conflicting feelings about Germans in many parts of the country. When the news broke that a prison camp was to be built in Handforth the locals were, according to *The Manchester Guardian*, very excited. The military had taken over the Dye works and a large company of Royal Engineers had begun to prepare it for prisoners. Some camps were already open and the prisoners at Newbury were described as performing acrobatics and dancing to the music of a man playing the mouth organ to entertain visitors. They also sang 'Tipperary', no doubt trying to impress the locals. Despite the obvious enjoyment of the prisoners they were made to collect their own firewood. Wounded German men at Frith Hill were reported to have said that they were well treated by the Allied medical services, while their own medics only treated officers. There was already accommodation for 5,000 prisoners at Frith Hill and a compound for another 10,000 was planned.

As well as the German prisoners, there were more refugees arriving in the country, this time from France. They had been on a steamer that hit a mine. There was bad feeling between them and the Belgians when they were admitted to Alexandra Palace and some violence broke out between them. There had already been some local problems with drunken Belgian refugees in the area who ended up in court. Later, there were recruits for the Belgian army from Canada housed in the palace.

The internment of civilians in Germany did not begin until after Britain had started the process. At the end of September there were still a number of British tourists free in Germany and, rather than interning them, it was reported that Thomas Cook and Sons were arranging for a representative to travel to Germany and bring them home. More serious violence towards foreign nationals was to occur much later.

October saw some serious outbreaks of violence in London. German owned shops were attacked and there were many arrests, but according to Rocker the real offenders were the yellow press. Shops were attacked in the Old Kent Road, Deptford, Brixton, and Poplar.

There had been a very uncertain beginning to internment in Britain, apart from the early victims who had been seen as dangerous. In October 1914, the military informed the Home Office that all male enemy aliens should be interned, except where it was undesirable. More early camps were set up at Aldershot, as well as at Douglas on the Isle of Man. Ships were also used early in the war as quarters for internees, but this often led to complaints from the German government. They were useful winter accommodation as they were easier to heat than camps. The ships also gave better-off internees the opportunity to pay for private cabins, which gave them more freedom. There were three internment ships moored off Southend in Essex early in the war. These were the *Royal Edward*, SS *Ivernia*, and the RMS *Saxonia*. The *Royal*

Edward had three classes of cabins, with various charges according to class and how many people shared a cabin. There was no issue with charging those interned for better accommodation, should they be able to afford it. Other ships were moored off the Isle of Wight: RMS *Tunisian*, the *Andania*, and the SS *Canada*. There were another three at Gosport, these were the *Scotian*, the *Lake Manitoba*, and the *Uranium*. Having prisoners in such a sensitive place as Portsmouth was not a good idea and they were only used until mid-1915.

Another problem that arose regularly in relation to internment was the lack of accurate identification of foreigners. When German artist Paul Cohen-Portheim arrived in England just before the war he had a passport, but thought it a ridiculous item as there was no need for passports in Europe. On the outbreak of war a German lady that he knew who lived in England went to the Russian embassy to try and change her German passport for a Russian one. This was because she was being treated badly thanks to her nationality. She saw nothing wrong in swapping her passport purely for her convenience. There was obviously not the same level of importance given to identification documents as there is today. There was so little need for a passport that most people did not have them. The exception was the Russians who needed a passport to leave their own country, not to get into other countries.

When war was declared, Cohen-Portheim, along with many other Germans and Austrians, had to report to police stations to register as an alien. The process did not seem to be well organised. There seemed to be little idea among the police of what was supposed to happen after this had taken place. When he went to stay with friends in Surrey, he later found out that this was not allowed, although no one had mentioned this restriction to him before. Cohen-Portheim also had no registration documents, because no one had remembered to give him any. Further investigation told him that he would need the permission of the Lord Lieutenant of the County of Surrey to be allowed to go there to visit his friends. The person he was going to visit was in fact the Lord Lieutenant. Although they were old friends, he felt uneasy while there—members of his friend's family joined the Army to fight in the war. He found that there was little antagonism displayed against foreigners by the population at first, although the feelings of the public gradually began to change, supported and egged on by many of the popular newspapers of the time, which were encouraging the internment of foreigners. The spy mania that erupted from time to time seemed to be connected with things going wrong with the British war effort. However, most foreign nationals were free to carry on living at home early in the war, although they were supposedly under observation by the police.

Despite the fact that so-called German spies had been under observation since well before the war, of those that had been arrested in early August none had actually been charged. Despite this, the number of suspicious aliens being held by this time numbered around 9,000. Apart from those under suspicion of spying, the government was doing little to address the matter of foreign nationals, so the public began to take matters into their own hands. Many employers who had not already done so dismissed their alien employees, with Austrian and German waiters being dismissed from the Savoy, Claridges, Berkeley, and Strand Palace hotels, and Lyons and Palmerston restaurants. On a more official level, the chief constable of Brighton served notice on all Germans and Austrians in the town to leave in October 1914, while Norfolk Council issued a notice that the whole county was prohibited to Belgian refugees—this was despite the fact that Belgium was an ally.

The vigorous public debate about what should happen to enemy aliens was often led by politicians. Mr Joynson-Hicks MP led a discussion at the Constitutional Club on the 'spy peril'. He praised the government over their running of the Army and Navy, but said that they were neglecting the danger posed by spies and that it was not always the suspect who was the most dangerous, but someone who appeared innocent. He called for all enemy aliens to be moved at least 20 miles from the coast, and either cleared out of the country or interned. Another MP, James Campbell, is recorded as saying that the time had come when every German should be told 'we cannot trust you'.

As well as registering enemy aliens there were further measures put in place—everyone who kept pigeons in the country had to be registered as well. It was an attempt to stop the use of carrier pigeons being sent to the continent with messages. By early October there seems to have been no unified government action in regard to enemy aliens. Scotland Yard issued a statement that no new instructions had been issued in regard to aliens in London. Meanwhile in other towns throughout the country widespread arrests were still taking place. Manchester seemed to be leading the action with hundreds of Germans being arrested on 21 October.

In late October, the London County Council made a representation to the government that it was highly undesirable that large numbers of alien enemies (who had been discharged from their jobs) should have free access to all parts of the capital. As they were in the most part destitute, they had to try and find places to sleep and food to eat. There was at last an attempt at a unified approach when the military told the government that something had to be done; some enemy aliens of military age, between seventeen and forty-five, were arrested and taken to clearing stations. According to *The Times*, there were 70,000 registered enemy aliens in the country—40,000 in London alone—and those from all walks of life were taken into custody.

The constant changes in regulations made things difficult for those involved in trying to help aliens in need. No sooner had the Society of Friends mastered the regulations, they would change. According to their report, Government policy appeared to be controlled by a jingoistic press. By the end of the month, the press in Germany were making incredible claims as to the situation in Britain. The *Cologne Gazette* claimed that Englishmen who employed German servants were imprisoned. The newspaper also claimed to have interviewed a man who was held in a stable at Newbury with 1,300 other Germans; allegedly his conditions had no furniture or lights and he had to sleep on straw and was fed only thin soup. They were calling for similar treatment for British subjects in Germany. In reply to this, *The Times* published an article in mid-November reproducing a report from the American embassy in London, whose representatives had examined the accommodation of the Germans interned in Britain. It was a very positive report and had been completed in early October, which would seem to point out that the report had been in German hands when they were writing the stories in the press criticising conditions for internees.

There had been some problems at the Newbury camp though. It was based at the race track and many of the internees had slept in stables and horse boxes at first, so there probably was some truth in the reports in the German press, but conditions improved at the camp as it became better organised.

By October 1914, nearly 1,000 Germans and Austrians had been arrested in London. Of these around 900, mainly waiters and hairdressers, were sent to Frith Hill by special trains from London and Brighton, raising numbers at the camp to around 9,000. A number of suspected spies were then moved from Frith Hill, Aldershot, which had been set up as an internment camp and later became a POW camp to the Isle of Man.

November saw the execution of the first German spy at the Tower of London. There had been a number of executions in France of German spies, but such actions were more likely to be carried out instantly in a battlefield situation. However, in England things were done properly and the spy had a trial before he was executed. Carl Hans Lody was a lieutenant in the German naval reserve. He had been sent to England at the outbreak of war, but had had no training in espionage. He claimed to be an American who had lost his passport. It was only five weeks later that he was arrested with details of cruisers in the North Sea. He became the first person executed in the tower for 150 years—Lody was the first, but not the last.

Although only one of the thousands of so-called suspicious aliens detained so far was a spy, it did little to change the public perception of the danger that foreign nationals posed. There definitely seems to have still been an air of panic over the presence of aliens in the country, despite the steps already taken. In November the matter was raised in the House of Lords, when it was claimed by the Earl of Crawford that petrol exportation from Fife could be a life or death matter if it was used to fuel an enemy ship. He also said that there was constant signalling taking place from that part of the coast. There had been a man charged with this offence.

There often seemed to be little distinction amongst the press or the public over those enemy aliens who could be a risk and those who were not; many saw anyone with a foreign name as a potential enemy. The problem the government had was that it was not as simple as that. Many Austrians were in fact Slavs who had greater sympathies with Russia than Germany and there were Poles from Prussia who were also mainly anti-German. Among those interned early were men with no financial means, men who had lived in England for years and who had worked until war was declared, who were then dismissed from their employment because they were foreign. It was this that had resulted in their lack of finance.

In November work was beginning on an old Jute factory in Stratford, east London, to turn it into an internment camp. A hundred men worked there for three weeks to get the factory ready to be what was called in the local press, comfortable winter quarters with slipper and spray baths. There were also cells included in case any of the prisoners should cause problems. A number of criminal charges were being brought against foreigners at this time. A German steeplejack was charged at Merthyr with preparing a document intended to be of use to the enemy, and inciting another person to commit an offence under the Official Secrets Act. He had approached someone, and tried to get him to send plans for a land mine to the German ambassador in America he was remanded in custody. In another incident, a radio equipment was discovered in a house overlooking the Firth of Forth, which could have been used to signal to any German ships that entered the harbour. No doubt this was what led to the Earl of Crawford's comments in the House of Lords. One very unusual charge against an enemy alien was that he failed to notify the authorities of his change of address. What was strange about this was that Harry Landberg, an Austrian, was a private in the Essex Regiment based at Colchester. His change of address was due to a move to the barracks in the town. He was sent to prison for six months.

Another case in Stratford, east London, with Frederick Roberts, a telephone inspector, charged with failing to register as an alien. Roberts was well known in the area as he was the champion walker of Essex. He was employed as a telephone inspector at Wanstead telephone exchange. Roberts claimed that, until 1905, he had believed himself to be British. It was only when he applied for his birth certificate that he found out he was Austrian and his real name was Deigel. As his employers knew that he was Austrian he expected this information to have been made known when the government took over the exchange, so he did not think that he had to register. The magistrate was quite enlightened, considering the feelings in the country at that time. He told Roberts that he was not one of those who thought that anyone born in an enemy country was dangerous. However, due to Roberts important job in which he could intercept messages, he sent him to prison for three months.

Internment was not only suffered by civilians. The early battles in Antwerp had involved the British Naval Brigade and many of them had accidentally crossed the border into Holland. Being a neutral power, the Dutch were forced to intern the men. The locals treated the men in a similar fashion to how the public at home had treated German prisoners—handing them gifts. Many of the men were living at Leewarden, where they were reportedly being well treated by the Dutch. They spent much of their time exercising and playing football in a similar fashion to the German military prisoners in Britain. They obviously had a better time in confinement than their comrades captured by the enemy.

Aliens were being gathered in several clearing stations around the country by late 1914. In Birmingham around seventy were in custody. Many of these men had English wives and families who had to apply for relief from the parish as their breadwinner had been taken away. In Leeds around 1,000 prisoners were being held in Lofthouse Park, with more arriving every day. At Newcastle eighty-five aliens were being held at the police station.

In November what had been the peaceful internment of aliens came to an end when five internees were shot dead at Douglas Camp and fifteen were wounded. They were being guarded by 300 men of the National Reserve and the Manx Territorials, commanded by Colonel Madoc. Relations between the prisoners and guards had become strained. The first incident to occur was when prisoners refused to leave the dining hall and go back to their tents because it was raining. A few days later there was a demonstration over the quality of the food, during which items were thrown around by the prisoners. They then made an attempt to rush the kitchens. A similar disturbance took place again a few days later and the internees again tried to rush the kitchen and threw things at the guards. Threats with bayonets and firing over the prisoners' heads did not stop them, so the guards fired into them. The five dead were Richard Fobs, a waiter from the Grand Hotel, Brighton; Richard Matthias, a sailor from a sunken German ship; Bernhard Warning, an engineer from the London Docks; Christian Brochl, a waiter from London; and Ludwig Bauer of Württemberg. The inquests found that the shootings were justified because of the riotous behaviour of the internees. The coroner at the inquest said that in his opinion the aliens detained in Douglas were prisoners of war. This then meant that they were subject to the rules of the camp. Colonel Madoc stated that he was sure that agitators had begun the trouble and tried to make speeches. Madoc was not present at the time of the shooting, but had arrived just after it happened. There were a number of men from the National Reserve involved in the incident, but also some volunteers had entered the dining hall. There was some uncertainty over whether anyone had given the order to fire or not. Some of those involved claimed they heard the order to fire, but Sargent Hammond, who was in command, said that there was no order, although he admitted shooting at one of the men that seemed to be a ringleader. One must wonder if some of the inexperienced guards panicked, but this is conjecture on my part. One of the guards, Private John Blackburn, admitted shooting a prisoner who was about to attack a guard with a chair.

There were some statements by the prisoners themselves. Walter Caester said that he was told that something would happen on 10 November. Adolf Brummel, another internee, claimed that he was told that some of the internes were armed with revolvers. Colonel Madoc said that two revolvers were later handed in by the prisoners. A representative from the American embassy visited the camp a few days later and found conditions very satisfactory.

The suspicion that there were agitators trying to cause trouble was born out when one of the internees, Kurt Vausch, was later charged with trying to stir up disaffection in the camp. It was claimed that he told others to conceal their identification numbers, to reject their food, and prepare for something awful before the fatal shootings took place. He at first pleaded guilty, but on advice from his representative, Baron Von Hollenfer, changed his plea to not guilty.

There would seem to have been some problems at the camp, which the American inspection may have glossed over in their report. It was also said that Colonel Madoc, the commandant who was also the Chief Constable of the Isle of Man, had been involved in the use of concentration camps during the Boer war and may have been too strict in carrying out his duties. Things did improve after the riot and those who could afford to pay got half a tent for twelve and six, or a third of a hut for 12s. There was also work available for those who wanted it, with a brush factory being set up at Douglas and one at Islington. Sewing machines were made by internees at Hackney, to replace the ones that had previously been made in Germany.

By the time of the riot at Douglas it had already been decided that another camp would be built on the Isle of Man, on a farm known as Knockaloe Moar. The site had been used as a Territorial Army camp in the past. Building began and Lieutenant Colonel J. M. Carpendale was appointed as commandant. Prisoners began to arrive as soon as some of the huts were finished. The original plan had been for the camp to hold 5,000 prisoners, this was continually added too until it held more than 20,000.

The writer H. G. Wells wrote an article as to how the war would change England. He gave a list of things, such as pictures of men in silk hats, soldiers in busbys and red coats, or even of a cricket bat, that would remind people of the good old times. There is often a romantic idea of the wonderful summer days before the war began, which seems to be what Wells is referring to. This ideal was no doubt the view of the upper classes who were the ones writing about such pleasant memories. It is doubtful that the families living in poverty in London's east end and in slum's in other parts of the country or those in workhouses had such rosy memories of the supposedly sunny pre-war days.

As well as an increasing number of internees, more German military prisoners were arriving in the country to fill new camps. One of the early camps for German military prisoners was at Leigh, Lancashire, in a mill building that had only recently been completed. When it was taken over, cottages that had been erected for the workers at the mill were used as billets for the camp guards. The decision to use the complex was taken in late 1914, not long after the war had begun, and there were plans to use it both for prisoners of war and civilian internees. Preparations were reported in detail in the local newspaper, the *Leigh Chronicle*. There was little of the secrecy that was to become the norm during the Second World War, although when the camp opened part of the road leading to it was closed to the public. It was well guarded because of the mutiny on the Isle of Man, which had led to fears of more unrest. The guards were to be 100 men of the National Reservists, commanded by Colonel Hawkins, who would march along with the prisoners with bayonets fixed. At the end of November it was reported that 2,000 prisoners would be arriving.

It appears that local newspapers were as ready to promote bad feeling against the enemy as the national press, and missed no chance to do so. An article in the *Leigh Chronicle* stated that the government had bought Donington Hall, Leicestershire, for £13,000, in order to use it as an officers' prison camp. Using a stately home for prisoners was just the kind of story to anger the public, giving them the idea that the prisoners lived in luxury. The *Chronicle* went on to inquire if the time had arrived when the government should be asked if British prisoners of war were to receive better treatment or whether German prisoners should be treated worse.

There were reports of disorder at the internment camp at Lancaster in early December, which had been reported as being put down with a bayonet charge by the guards. There seemed to be some dispute over the facts of what happened, but it seems that the dispute began after a fight between a Frenchman (who had been told he was to be released) said he would join the French army and fight the Germans and some of the German internees took offence to this. *The Manchester Guardian* printed a statement by the camp commandant Lieutenant Colonel Ansley; he admitted that a fight had taken place between some of the internees, but said that no one had been injured by a bayonet charge. Although the alarm bell had been rung and the soldiers had assembled, this was due to a mistake in the setting off of the fire alarm. The disorder was in no way due to grievances about conditions in the camp. The Frenchman at Lancaster was not the only man to be released. It seems that some of the early arrests may have been due to over eager application of the new alien rules. An Austrian man who had been held at Queensferry had also been released and had written to *The Manchester Guardian* to say how well he had been treated in the camp and by his English friends now that he was free again.

Disturbances amongst those interned were quite common and not just in Britain. When Antwerp fell to the Germans a large number of Belgian soldiers, along with a number of members of the British naval brigade, managed to escape to Holland. Some of the Belgians managed to reach England and re-joined the Army. In line with the Dutch rules on neutrality the rest were interned. There was unrest at the camp near Zeist after some Belgians tried to escape. There was already some disquiet over this and then the wives of some of the men were turned away when they tried to visit. There were around 12,000 prisoners in the camp and when visits were again refused the prisoners attacked the guards who opened fire, killing six of the prisoners and injuring many more.

Rudolf Rocker was arrested in early December and after spending one night in Leaman Street police station was taken to Olympia. Most of the press reports on the early camp at Olympia suggest that it was a pleasant camp where the internees were quite relaxed. Rocker told a different story. Taken before the commandant Lord Lanesborough, he was asked if he would like to stay in the restaurant. It was where the best people lived and paid £1 a week for the privilege, he refused—not surprising when one considers his socialist beliefs.

The main camp consisted of two halls; in one hall, according to Rocker, there were a number of men breaking stones. The whole room was full of dust and they were guarded by men with fixed bayonets. This is the first report I have seen of internees being forced to perform hard labour. The second hall was the living quarters. Visitors were often forced to wait outside for hours and only allowed in for three minutes. The conditions were poor with no place to dry clothes. There were only five toilets and five wash basins for 1,200 men. Guards hurried the queues for the toilets with jabs from fixed bayonets.

Rocker was in camp twelve, which was just one section of the hall divided by ropes. Those in his camp were better off than others. They had their own straw sacks to sleep on. Those in other camps had to break stones and had to pile their straw sacks up during the day, which meant that they had a different one every night. The food was poor and there was never enough of it. There was also no heating in the halls.

There were more problems at Douglas in December when one of the internees, Otto Luz, was charged with breaches of camp regulations. He had written a letter to his sister in Germany using invisible ink, to ask for details of how the war was proceeding. He also made a number of, what were said to be false, claims about conditions in the camp, criticising the food and saying that the 25,000 internees could easily attack the guards.

As the first Christmas of the war approached, *The Times* published a story saying that more than 12,000 parcels had arrived for both POWs and internees from relatives in Germany. A large amount of money had also been sent. The report also stated that many of those in the civilian camps were not there because they were seen as a danger to the country, but had applied to enter the camps. These were mainly men who were destitute and chose the camps over the workhouse.

Despite the call to arrest all aliens of military age in October, there had been little more done to deal with the rest of those seen to be enemy aliens. One reason for this may have been the increase of enemy military prisoners entering the country and a lack of available camps and guards for these and the civilian aliens. The majority of those of German, Austrian, and Hungarian extraction were still free by the end of the year. It was a situation that was to lead to problems for the government in the following year. As the end of the year approached the populations of many towns in the country changed dramatically, as large army camps appeared in places where they had not been before. Small villages, such as Rainham, Essex, with a population of a few hundred, were suddenly swamped by the inhabitants of an enormous tented camp by the small army barracks at Purfleet. The populations of many towns exploded as civilians were outnumbered by soldiers. In Southend there were a number of new arrivals just before Christmas. A thousand German military prisoners marched through the town on their way to take their berths on the prison ships moored off the pier. Many of the men were described as carrying what looked like Christmas hampers. One of these was Rudolf Rocker who had been transferred from Olympia to Southend.

The populations of other seaside towns were not as lucky as those at Southend where the Germans they saw were already harmless. Although air raids had not yet begun, Scarborough, Whitby, and Hartlepool were attacked by German ships on the 16 December. The towns were shelled by the German ships. A number of buildings were destroyed and some people killed. This included the first soldier killed on British soil by an enemy since 1665.

Hartlepool did actually have three forts and was a protected port. The forts were poorly armed, with only five guns between them. There were five German ships involved, the *Blücher*, the *Seydlitz*, the *Moltke*, the *Drefflinger*, and the *Von der Tann*. The fact that Britannia supposedly ruled the waves did not deter the enemy ships from attacking and two British destroyers, the *Doon* and the *Hardly*, and the gunboat *Patrol* tried to intervene during the shelling and were quickly fought off. The German ships may have been firing on the forts and the ship yards, but many of the shells went over them and into the town.

When Rocker arrived at Southend he said that the locals lined the streets hurling abuse and that if they had not been guarded they would have been lynched. Rocker seemed to be under the impression that the town had suffered a fatal air raid the evening before they arrived. He was mistaken in this as the only air raid to occur in December took place at Dover. Rocker was taken out to the *Royal Edward* moored off the pier. He was lucky in that some of the prisoners were sent to the *Saxonia*, which was not as pleasant a ship. He found the ship an improvement on Olympia, especially after he was given a cabin that he shared with one other man. The worst aspect of the ship was being forced to stand on deck for three hours to be counted whatever the weather.

Although visitors were allowed on the ship, they had to pay for the fare from London to Southend and had to find their own boat to take them out to the ship. Rocker watched his wife being almost flung from a small boat one day, until eventually she had to give up because the weather was too bad for her to climb aboard. On the ship the guards were more considerate, and there were better washing facilities than at Olympia—there were even baths with hot water. The food was better, though still not very good and there was not enough of it. Rocker was once reprimanded for writing to his wife that the only thing on sale in the canteen was tobacco not food. When some high ranking Germans arrived on the ship they were given the best cabins as they paid for them. They were also given better food and had exclusive use of the upper deck, which had once been used for all internees. The men were led by a Baron von Nettleheim and did not wish to mix with the rest of the men on the ship.

There had been attempts to exchange prisoners from early in the war, but as it was thought that the war would not last for long these did not begin to be taken seriously until much later. Another problem was that there were also practical difficulties in the arrangement of transport for exchanged men.

2

1915

The year of 1915 was to see some new developments in the war. The Germans began to bomb the Allied countries from their large airships and also used poison gas for the first time against the Russians on the Eastern Front. Gas was used again against the British at the second Battle of Ypres. The year was also to see the ill-fated landing of colonial troops at Gallipoli, and Italy entered the war on the Allied side. If the use of gas and the bombing of civilians had not done enough to turn the world against the Germans, then the sinking of the *Lusitania* and the shooting of the British nurse Edith Cavell certainly did. Despite the outcry at the German use of gas, there was a lower key event when the British used it for the first time, especially after it blew back on our own troops. Douglas Haig became the commander of the British forces.

The beginning of 1915 had seen an increase in food prices, which were of course a struggle for the working classes despite the higher wages that the war had brought. The price of wheat had risen dramatically by more than 70 per cent; meat had also risen in price. So many fishermen had joined the Navy that fish was in short supply and also expensive. It wasn't only food prices that had risen, many miners had enlisted in the forces so coal prices also rose.

The rise in wages during the war is often given as proof of improved living conditions among the working class. This was true in homes where there were a number of workers. It was often a different situation in homes where only one person worked or where none did. There were also many homes where the main breadwinner had joined the forces, so high wages did not improve their situation as it did not apply to the forces.

The first prisoners had arrived at Stratford just before Christmas and by January there were around 100 in the camp; some of these were military prisoners of war. There was less of a difference between military and civilian camps early in the war. The commandant of Stratford was Colonel De Burke. The local newspaper the *Stratford Express* had an unusual story, which claimed that no one knew about the camp, even those whose houses surrounded it. This was despite the same newspaper having published a story about the camp being prepared in the previous November.

The number of British prisoners held in Germany quickly outstripped the number held in any previous wars. By early 1915 the country already had over half a million Allied prisoners, not including civilians—there were 8,138 officers and 577,876 other ranks. The British prisoners numbered 492 officers and 18,823 of other ranks; the total included French, Russians, and Belgians. The treatment of British prisoners was often criticised, both for the lack of food they were given and the harsh punishments that were dished out; the former was often explained by the shortage of German supplies. There did seem to be a case for the reality of mistreatment of British prisoners. There were many cases of abuse of Germany's prisoners from other Allied countries, but it seemed to be the English prisoners who suffered the most. The Germans were believed to have more regard for the French prisoners that they held. It was not all British prisoners who were treated badly; the Irish, who were then still part of Britain, were treated much better, although there may have been a reason for this. Many of them were held in a separate Irish camp at Limberg and were allowed a visit from an ex-British consul general, Sir Roger Casement. The more lenient treatment may have had its basis in the hope that the Irish could be tempted to join Casement's Irish Brigade and fight against the English. A plan that wasn't very successful, as very few took the opportunity to do so. This leniency towards the Irish may not have been an isolated case. When Morgan's book on German atrocities was later published, he claimed in it that no atrocities took place against Indian troops; when captured, German officers told them that they harboured no bad feelings towards them and that they should not fight against German troops. They were also asked to bring their comrades over to fight on the German side. One Indian soldier interviewed by Morgan claimed that the Germans had offered him money and land to change sides.

There were some English prisoners who believed that the treatment the Germans inflicted on them was no different to how German officers treated their own men. It was part of German culture to treat their soldiers harshly and the soldiers responded by treating their prisoners in a similar way. I do think that there is some truth in this view, but there were cases when the treatment of British prisoners went beyond this. The treatment in a camp was also dependant on the commandant. In Scneidemuhl Camp, the prisoners were often beaten by the guards, though when a new commandant took over the beatings were stopped and conditions in the camp improved enormously. Not all camps were bad; one small officer's camp at Blankenburg was described by Mr J. B. Jackson of the American embassy as the equal of any camp in Britain.

There were some enemy aliens who were allowed to leave Britain early in the war, after the permits were introduced, but these were mainly women. This included a number of young ladies who had been at a summer school in Oxford when war broke out—a few of them were teachers. Others allowed to leave were women whose husbands were interned and the majority of these were helped by the Society of Friends. The journey back to Germany was not an easy one, there were a number of rumours about the terrible conditions of the railways in Europe. It was believed that the railways at the frontiers had been destroyed. There were also rumours of agents of the white slave trade infesting the trains in Holland. Travelling for young women was a different proposition at this time. There was a man who was sending letters to young German girls saying that their father's had asked him to bring them home. This may have only been a financial trick as he was asking them for £10 for the journey, which only cost around 30s, though there could have been a more sinister motive.

It was not only the journey across Europe that was to be a test for them. At Folkestone there were lengthy examinations as to who was allowed to leave the country; often the regulations had been changed between the time of the aliens setting out from home and their arriving at a British port. Those not allowed to leave often had to spend the night in waiting rooms, with there being no other accommodation available.

The claims that all aliens were being well cared for in Britain did not stand up to closer examination. One family, with four children under four, had their father interned. While this was happening his wife died, with the youngest child only two weeks old; it took weeks to arrange the necessary permits to allow the children to be taken back to Germany. An American doctor agreed to accompany them, but actually ended up with eight children to take home, seven of them under six years of age.

Despite constant claims of mistreatment by Germans towards British prisoners, there was a society operating in German on similar lines to the Society of Friends at home. The Committee for the Advice and Assistance of Germans Abroad and Foreigners in Germany continued its work throughout the war, helping those seen as enemy aliens. The society cared for the families of a number of interned men. They also sent parcels to British POWs in Germany who had received none from home. They arranged to repatriate a number of children from Belgium and France who had been separated from their parents due to the war, as well as trying to find their parents.

There were reports in the German press that the prisoners in Britain were not allowed to celebrate the Kaiser's birthday. This was refuted in *The Times* at the end of January when they reported on the camp at Stratford. The interior was decked out with German and Austrian colours. The inmates were wearing souvenir badges and a concert was held at which German music was played. There was a report published in February 1915 by the International Red Cross in Geneva, which had sent Professor Eduard Naville and Monsieur Victor Van Bercham to inspect British POW camps. The report confirmed comments made by other inspectors. Out of thousands of German prisoners interviewed none were dissatisfied with the food or their treatment. In Holyport Camp the inspectors found around fifty prisoners in a room chatting or reading, with a large Christmas tree dominating the room. In the dining hall a large German flag was hanging on the wall.

There was one inspector, Mr Goudsmit of Copenhagen, who was allowed access to both German and British camps. He said that the German camp at Ruhleben was satisfactory, that the food was good, and that 80 per cent of the prisoners had beds, but he believed that this was now the case for all prisoners. Food was also available for sale to prisoners. Concerts were put on, with a small entrance charge and the money was given to the poorer prisoners. Goudsmit described the treatment of German prisoners in England as splendid, after visiting four camps. Dorchester, which was a military camp, had a commanding officer, Major Bulkeley, who was positively popular amongst the prisoners. They were in barracks, but huts were being built to extend the size of the camp. It appeared as if the German military prisoners in Britain were quite happy with their situation. Those who had been in the Army or Navy would have been more used to the discipline in camps and would not have felt the injustice suffered by many civilian internees who felt that they had done nothing wrong. There may have also been a view that they were better off where they were than in the trenches.

The German admiralty declared a blockade of Britain in February, which meant that their submarines would attack merchant ships including those of neutral countries. According to the *War Illustrated* it was one of the rules of war that no merchant ship, even if it belonged to an enemy, should be sunk or appropriated. That they were prepared to use their U-boats to sink merchant ships was described as Hunnishness.

At West Ham Police Court in February, William Stevens was charged with being an alien in a prohibited area—the Rank Flour Mill at Victoria Dock London. Stevens had been a foreman at the mill for ten years and was said to be a very reliable man. It was unusual for an alien to still be employed at this stage of the war. Mr Jackson, the clerk of the court, asked if he was paid the same wages as English workers and if English workers were not competent to do his job.

There were a number of claims made by internees of items being stolen from them by soldiers at various camps, yet nothing came of their claims. If civilians stole from them, then action did seem to be taken. In March three men appeared at Stockport Court—William Edginton, Robert Brookshaw, and Wilfred Jackson—all charged with theft. It was claimed that the men stole from packages belonging to internees at Handforth Camp. The owners of the goods had arrived at Handforth Station and been taken to the camp. The next day their luggage followed and they found a number of items missing. Edgington and Brookshaw were porters at the station; Jackson was the son of a local farmer who had a contract to deliver goods from the station to the camp. After the prisoners reported the missing items, the railway police investigated and the three men had admitted the theft. One of the items was a purse that Jackson had sold for 4*d*. The two prisoners whose items had been stolen were allowed to attend the court under armed guard. The prosecutor for the London and North Western Railway said that 'no one in this country wishes to have it said that we have copied the example of our enemies in Belgium and elsewhere'. It was the first case of this kind, despite the large amount of luggage that was moved between the station and the camp. They were all fined 20*s* or fourteen days.

The fact that the people being interned were mainly married men with families did not seem to worry those calling for all aliens to be interned. How these men, who had been living blameless lives in Britain for many years, may have felt at being dragged away from their families and locked up did not seem to have any bearing on their treatment.

Herman Krauss was a married man with three children. He was thirty-nine years of age and had been a waiter at a hotel until he was arrested and sent to Lofthouse Camp in the previous October. He was described by a friend who had known him seventeen years to have been a quiet reserved man. As those arrested this early were supposed to have been the most dangerous, Krauss did not seem to fit the description. After his internment he had become more reserved and would not speak to anyone. One Saturday morning he had approached another prisoner and said goodbye to him. The man asked if he was being released and was told yes, a very good release. An hour later he was found dead in a lavatory where he had killed himself. It is impossible to tell how many other men felt suicidal after being separated from their families, especially after having done nothing wrong apart from being born in another country.

Many of the men who had been sent to Stratford early in the war were moved in March. There was a group of 400 who marched from the camp to the station on their way to the Isle of Man. They were strongly guarded and the group included some Turkish officers—there were still military men and civilians in the same camps.

The arrival of Gunther Plüschow in Gibraltar in April was to be the beginning of an amazing escapade by him. The German officer had already escaped from captivity in China and made his way to America and then by ship to Gibraltar on his way back to Germany. He was posing as a Swiss national, though he was suspected of being German by the authorities and imprisoned with other German internees in a prison. All the inmates of the prison in Gibraltar used to house internees were then put aboard a British troopship on its way to England. Realizing by this time that his claim to be Swiss was pointless, Plüschow admitted to being a German officer, hoping for better treatment. The ship's captain offered him better accommodation if he promised not to try and escape—Plüschow refused. After landing at Plymouth, Plüschow was taken by train to Portsmouth with some other prisoners. They were locked in a cold room, but bribed the guards to bring them food and firewood. The next morning they were taken out to the prison ships moored off the Isle of Wight and being used as internment camps. The officer in charge on the first ship refused to take them and they were eventually taken aboard the *Andania* following an argument between officers on the ship and those transporting them. Plüschow claimed that the commandant of the ship was a man who had bought his commission before the war and instead of treating him like an officer, he kept him locked up to stop him from escaping. He was also put on short rations in retaliation for the way British prisoners were being treated in Germany.

If what Plüschow said was true, then it sounds as if the constant claims that no retaliation was used against German prisoners may have been the government plan, but that it was not followed by all those officers who were in command of the camps. As it was in Germany, conditions in British camps depended largely of the commandant. Plüschow even claimed that the commandant offered a separate dining area and better food to prisoners if they paid him.

Shortly after his arrival, Plüschow was transferred to Dorchester camp. The camp had once been an army base and had originally been used for civilian prisoners and sailors, but later military prisoners had been added. He found the camp much better than the ship and was treated well. He was even given his own room as he was the only officer in the camp. The number of guards had been doubled at Leigh camp in February when the first prisoners arrived. They came by train and were marched through the town, which aroused a great deal of interest among the locals. Not much bad feeling was reported, in fact many gave the prisoners gifts of cigarettes and fruit.

Despite this, the local newspaper *Leigh Chronicle* did not refrain from reminding the locals that these men were responsible for the murder of Belgian and French women and children. One article also stated that the prisoners would be well housed, while British prisoners in Germany were half starved and treated like dogs. Even the local press was happy to create bad feeling against the enemy, even those who were already in captivity. Although the public was not allowed near the camp, a representative from the *Leigh Chronicle* was. He reported that reveille was at 7 a.m., followed by breakfast at 8.30 a.m. Dinner was at 12.30 p.m. and tea at 5 p.m., and the prisoners had to be in bed by 10 p.m. Heads of messes, elected by the prisoners, played the part of prefects and wore badges of rank; they were the intermediaries between the guards and the prisoners.

Much of the prisoners' time was spent playing football or other outdoor sports, while card games were played inside. There was also a library of German books available. The men were allowed two censored letters a week, and letters and parcels were authorised from friends. There was also a canteen where food could be purchased.

Those who were willing to work were paid between 5s and 7s a week for their labour.

The feeling in Leigh, supported by the *Chronicle*, was that the prisoners would not try and escape even if the gates were left open because they were so happy there. This was proved wrong on 9 April when Friedrich Schwenke walked out of the gate dressed as a civilian. He was arrested at a railway station in Manchester a few hours later, before anyone at the camp had even noticed him missing.

Some German prisoners were happy with where they found themselves. A letter was sent from a group of seamen in Handforth Camp. They were survivors of the *Blücher*, which had been sunk in the battle of Dogger Bank in January. The letter was to their captors and was printed in *The Times*. They wrote that they had initially been taken to Edinburgh Castle where they received good reception and were given clothes. They were then sent to Handforth, near Manchester, where they had enough to eat, plenty of light and air, but very little to smoke.

Captured German officers were to be sent to a camp at Donington Park, Leicestershire, which was the property of Mr Frederick Gretton. The government had spent £20,000 in adapting the camp, which was a stately home set in 400 acres of wooded parkland. The camp itself was based in 20 acres adjoining the hall. This was surrounded by an 8-foot barbed wire fence set 3 feet into the ground. The use of a stately home attracted a lot of adverse press attention. A group of MPs visited Donington Hall to see for themselves what it was like. They were shown around by the commandant Captain Aldridge accompanied by a guard with fixed bayonets. They saw the house as well as the new dormitories that had been built, and met several of the prisoners. There had already been trouble at Donington, when the interned men who had been sent to the camp to act as valets were rude and abusive towards the officers. The officers complained to the commandant, and as a result two of the valets were returned to their camp at Wakefield.

There had been claims in the German press about bad treatment of men at a camp at Newbury the previous year. *The Times* published an account of the camp by a former prisoner. He described it as having three compounds; one consisted of stables and the other two of tents. The guards only entered the compounds if they needed to carry messages and were unarmed. The compounds were run by the prisoners themselves so, with no guards in the compounds, it was hard to see how there had been any mistreatment apart from living conditions in the camp, which had been quite basic at first. The claims by the Germans of mistreatment were quickly countered by similar claims by the British press as to the mistreatment of British prisoners in Germany. The *War Illustrated* published a full page drawing of a wounded British officer being verbally abused by German soldiers. The story accompanying the picture described the mistreatment as men being transported in horse boxes on trains. These were still covered in horse droppings. There were also a number of stops made and cases of verbal abuse by soldiers and civilians.

The internment of civilians did not only apply to enemy aliens who lived in Britain. When the British invaded German colonies in East Africa, the German civilians living there were taken prisoner. In scenes very similar to reports of what occurred in the Boer War, the civilians were taken during the night and were not allowed to take any more than they were wearing, which in many cases were nightclothes. There seems no reason why they would not be allowed to take their clothes with them, or at the very least be allowed to dress first. This could have been seen as a claim of mistreatment by the Germans, but in fact the internees were sent to England and when they arrived they still had few clothes. Thirty of the men had been sent to a camp in England. The Society of Friend sent clothes for them, which were returned by the commandant. A few months later they received a letter from the commandant of the camp asking for more clothes for some scantily clad men from the tropics.

Prisoners were still being kept on ships as well as on land. These ships had also been used for civilian internees, but they were expensive for the government that hired them. The hire of nine ships was costing between £7,000 and £12,500 a month, depending on the size of the ship. By this time three of the ships had been taken out of service. The remaining six held the following numbers of prisoners: *Ascania*, 1,397; *Scotian*, 1,132; *Lake Manitoba*, 1,242; *Saxonia*, 2,300; *Ivernia*, 1,575; and *Royal Edward*, 1,200. Each ship cost between £1,000 and £1,500 to fit out. As places for the prisoners became available on shore the ships were retired.

Although the majority of German military and naval prisoners found themselves in camps there was one exception. This was German U-boat crews. They were not seen as honourable prisoners and were sent to the naval detention barracks at Chatham. Although treated well, they were kept in cells at night. This caused some dispute in Britain as although U-boat crews were seen as murderers of civilians aboard the ships they sank, another view was that they were only following orders. Their imprisonment was influenced by Winston Churchill who wanted them held separately. There was also a problem over the U-boat crews in that the Germans retaliated by keeping some British officers in Germany in solitary confinement; they chose officers from distinguished families for this treatment. This action was not always accurate. Lieutenant French of the Royal Irish Regiment was included because he was thought to be related to Sir John French. They also thought that Lieutenant Baron Alliston's first name was actually a title. The men were sent to prisons in Cologne, Burg, or Madburg. Although the latter two were modern and conditions were quite good it was a different story at Cologne prison.

Winston Churchill was keen to continue with the plan to keep the crews separate from other prisoners, which, as they were being treated the same, did seem pointless—especially if it caused problems for British prisoners in Germany. The idea of keeping U-boat crews in separate accommodation was finally abandoned shortly after.

There is no doubt that this incident must have had an effect on later calls for reprisals against German prisoners, when British prisoners in Germany were reported as being mistreated. Inflicting more severe treatment on the German prisoners may have then led to even greater suffering for the British POWs. There was also a feeling that mistreating prisoners was not the English way, although not everyone agreed with this view. The treatment of both interned civilians and military prisoners in Britain seems to have been as reasonable as could be expected in the majority of cases. German officers were paid half the rate of similar ranks in the British forces while they were in captivity. Food was provided free, but they had to buy their own clothes and they were also allowed to buy alcohol. They were housed separately from the lower ranks in country houses or officer barracks and had servants. The lower ranks were also paid if they worked, but were given free food and clothing. They were mainly housed in barracks or other buildings, which were heated and had lights. Some were still housed in tents where there was no alternative, but this changed as better accommodation became available. They could buy tobacco and fruit, but not alcohol. Obviously other ranks were not to be trusted with alcohol while officers were.

There had been an agreement between Germany and France over wounded prisoners early in the war, but Britain was not included in this. Some of the wounded prisoners from both sides had been sent to Switzerland in January. The War Office had not agreed that British prisoners should be included, although this was eventually over ruled by the Foreign Office and an agreement to include the British wounded took place.

Despite the fact that a war was being fought in Europe there were what was seen as a number of unpatriotic events at home when workers went on strike for higher wages. There was a very interesting article published in the *War Illustrated* by Miss Marie Correlli entitled *Workers and Shirkers*. Miss Correlli gave some interesting hints as to her views. She blamed the lack of patriotism shown by workers on the long and splendid peace enjoyed in the country until now. This had created an atmosphere of comfort and security, which had engendered personnel selfishness. I doubt many working-class families would agree with her, with the threat of the workhouse looming over them should they fall ill or lose their job.

Naval action saw the German cruiser SMS *Dresden* sunk by the British cruisers HMS *Kent* and HMS *Glasgow*; the first information to reach the press following this event was how the British sailors rescued their drowning enemies from the sea. It further mentioned that these actions had not been reciprocated when the HMS *Good Hope* and the *Monmouth* had been sunk by the Germans in the previous November.

When Germany went to war with Britain it also went to war with its empire. What this meant to the countries that came under British rule was discussed by Mr Sidney Low, the lecturer on Imperial and Colonial History at King's College London. He believed that the war would solidify the sentiment of Imperial unity. The number of colonial troops who rallied to fight alongside the British in many theatres of war seems to prove his argument. Mr Low had obviously expected this to be the case with countries such as Australia, Canada, and New Zealand, but seemed to have been surprised at the reaction of what he described as the 'subject races of India, Egypt, and the Sudan'. There had been a belief in Germany that the populations of these places would have little interest in the war or in supporting Britain. This was not the case and large numbers of men from these countries did play their part in the war, aiding their colonial masters.

There were reports of two escaped prisoners in the press in early April. A £10 reward was offered for their capture and descriptions were given of the two men in the newspapers. The men were officers who had escaped from a camp in Denbighshire, which was situated in a country house owned by Lady Dundonald. The house was placed at the disposal of the Government by lady Dundonald at the outbreak of war. The camp held around 100 officers.

Later the same month two German officers, Lieutenant Von Sandersleben and Lieutenant Hans Ambler, were arrested at Llanbededr, a village on the coast of Cardigan Bay in Wales. The two men had escaped from Llansannan Camp in Denbighshire the previous week. A river watcher spotted the men acting suspiciously, and they did not reply when he spoke to them. He reported the men to a policeman who had been searching for the two Germans. When the policeman approached them they claimed to be French tourists. They put up no resistance when he handcuffed them, and after being taken to a police station they admitted to a justice of the peace that they were the escaped prisoners. They had money, food, and a map of the area in their possession. The two men later appeared before Fesiniog magistrates. There was reported to have been laughter in the court when it was said that the men had claimed to be French tourists. The prisoners did not seem to be put out by the court appearance and joined in with the laughter. There was more laughter when it was revealed that Audler had told the men who captured them that they did not like the camp and wanted to be sent to one near a submarine base. They were detained until a decision was made as to where they would be sent.

There were more escape attempts in April when a tunnel was discovered at a camp at Philberds, near Maidenhead. The adjutant of the camp, Captain Armstrong, was suspicious at the sudden interest shown in gardening by the prisoners. He ordered pipes to be laid near the garden and a tunnel was found. It had been cut through the concrete foundations of a high brick wall. The house held around 100 German officers and forty servants and were being guarded by the Devon Territorials. There had been a feeling that many of the military prisoners were happier to be held in captivity than to return to the trenches. The number of escapes and attempted escapes seems to go against this. It did seem that many of those trying to escape were officers, so perhaps they had a greater sense of duty and felt that they should try and return to the war.

The thought of keeping all prisoners locked in camps for the duration of the war was beginning to be questioned in some quarters There was an inquiry by the local council at Rothwell, near Wakefield, as to whether German prisoners at Lofthouse Park Camp could be used as labour to convert a piece of waste ground into a burial ground. They wanted to use around fifty men for eight or nine weeks, but wanted to know how much they would need to be paid and who would guard them. The idea of using prisoners outside their camps was not one that was popular early in the war.

By April 1915 there were more claims made about German spying. The MP Mr Joynson-Hicks was strongly anti-German and demanded once again, this time in the House of Commons, that all enemy aliens in London should be interned, either in workhouses or in the Crystal Palace. He also recommended that they should be moved from all sensitive areas, and that one minister should be responsible for them. In fact, since the previous November, the responsibility for the internment of enemy aliens had been that of the military. Lord Kitchener was not willing to relinquish the responsibility at the time.

In April the American ambassador went to the Halle Camp in Germany and was allowed into the camp, but he was not permitted to speak to prisoners without a German officer being present. There did seem to be more restrictions on the inspectors of German camps than there were on those inspecting camps in Britain who seemed to be given free access to all areas and all prisoners. The question of the treatment of prisoners in Britain and in Germany was often debated in the House of Commons. Before one debate there was an inspection by a commons delegation of several camps. The delegation received few complaints from prisoners, but found that conditions did vary between camps. At Stratford, east London, they found that the camp was run on democratic principles, with the leaders of each mess being elected. This seems to conflict with later views from internees. It was said that Stratford had a bad name among internees and that the staff there were very strict.

There was also some differences between internees held on ships. At Southend the internees were quite happy. On the *Royal Edward* they were divided into two classes—Baron's Court and Whitechapel. Paid 2s a day, members of Baron's Court were living as well as passengers on a first-class liner. Those on the ships moored off Ryde were not so happy; they had no visitors as Ryde was a restricted area and as their visitors were likely to also be aliens they were restricted from going there. The views of the delegation did not always seem to reflect the views of some internees. There were claims that the men paying for the best accommodation on the *Royal Edward* were being given the better conditions at the expense of the rest of the men held on the ship.

At Donington Hall the MPs met the senior German officer, Captain John Ross, who had been the commander of the *Blücher* and whose grandfather was Scottish. The captain spoke perfect English. The hall had a piano that the prisoners had bought themselves and the camp seemed pleasant. Duffryn Aled, North Wales, however, was described as gloomy, with iron bars on the windows; it had been a lunatic asylum. Other buildings used as camps included a dye works at Handsworth, a weaving shed at Leigh, a machine works at Lancaster, a distillery at Frongoch, and a workhouse at Oldcastle. One camp that was very different from others was Estcote Camp, near Blisworth. It was not under War Office control and was founded by the Destitute Aliens Committee. It mainly contained seamen and was run by Mr Havelock Wilson who was not a soldier or a policeman. He said that he was under the control of the Home Office, but it was not clear what his powers were. It was guarded by police officers, but the inmates were mainly there on a voluntary basis and numbered just under 800. There was another officer's camp at Holyport. It was situated in an old Victorian mansion that had been built on the site of the home of Nell Gwynne. It held 100 officers and forty other ranks who acted as servants. One of the recent arrivals was Gunter Plüschow who had finally been granted his wish to be placed in an officer's camp. The officers had their own beds and even had clean sheets. The food was cooked by German chefs taken off a liner and the prisoners were allowed wine and beer. A tailor visited every two weeks and there was regular post from Germany. Many of the prisoners were well-known men in their fields, such as Ferdinand Friedensburg the geologist and Dr Arnold Kohlschutter the astronomer.

Plüschow was not to enjoy the pleasures of Holyport for very long and was with a group of others who were transferred to Donington Hall. Until now the locals that Plüschow had seen in his journeys around the different camps had been either friendly or had ignored him. This changed at Donington and as they marched to the camp locals, mostly woman, booed them and threw countless objects at them. This was before the *Lusitania* was sunk, which was often given as the main event that changed the attitude of the British public to their German captives. Donington Hall was always a target for the press and according to the *Daily Mail* the officers were waited on and shaved by those captured from the ranks—this took place in oak-panelled rooms. *The New York Times* claimed that the ground floor of the mansion had been turned into a club and that numerous bathrooms had been installed in the building. What had often been described as a fine, old country house had in truth been declining for a number of years—it had stood empty for some time before the war. There were not enough bathrooms or kitchens for the vast number of men held there. The commandant was Lieutenant Colonel Francis Slater Picot, former commandant of a military prison, who like many other camp commandants had been brought out of retirement to run the camp. The advantage that Donnignton Hall had over Holyport was its grounds, which were large and allowed much more activity for the prisoners. The prisoners were allowed to wander in the grounds during the day, but were then locked into the smaller area of the night-time camp.

It was agreed in May that wounded British prisoners sent to Switzerland would be on parole. Any who escaped would be returned by the countries involved. There were many more German and French prisoners involved than British who were the most recent to participate in the scheme. The men were expected to work and it was thought that they would stay in Switzerland until the war ended.

The Manchester Guardian was not one of those newspapers that promoted anti-German feeling. In April, they published an article relating to the Distressed Foreigners Aid Society. They said that now that all those aliens who presented a danger had been interned it was only right that those who were not dangerous should be helped if they are unable to maintain themselves. Many of those who had not been interned had lost their jobs and were destitute. This also applied to the families of those who were interned. Any help from the government was, according to the society, hedged round with rules and complex points of nationality or marriage, which stopped many of them getting help. They must then be helped by charity and the Society was asking for funds to do this in Manchester.

The Home Secretary was still against wholesale internment at this time and argued it was impossible to claim that nationality was an offence. Bonar Law disagreed, arguing that every person of German birth should be treated with suspicion. He remarked that the starting point in any discussion should be the belief that enemy aliens would help their country against Britain if they got the chance. Sir Henry Dalziel argued that the government knew there was a settled spy system operating in Britain, and that many of these suspicious persons had escaped because of the overlapping authority of those responsible for them. All this was despite the fact that espionage had played no great part in any previous conflict.

The government were aware of the expense of providing new camps and of then having to help to support the families of the men who would be interned if those calling for the internment of all aliens got their way. There was also an awareness that the majority of those aliens still at large were not a source of danger to the country.

The use of Alexandra Palace as a home for Belgian refugees had been a decision that, if not applauded by locals, had been accepted due to the sympathy felt for them. When at the end of April the refugees had gone and the palace was again empty there was some hopes that it may have reopened to the public. This was not to happen. There were rumours that the palace may be used to house wounded British soldiers. The news that it was to become a camp for interned enemy aliens did not go down well locally. The first arrival of 500 prisoners took place in May; they included some military and naval prisoners. It became very difficult for anyone to get into the building—even the staff had their passes checked numerous times.

The War Office took over the building, and the rent that had been paid for the Belgians was reduced by £25 a week. The catering staff that had worked with the Belgians lost their jobs and £140 was given in compensation. The photography company that had its premises in the palace were given notice to quit. The local newspaper the *Hornsey Journal* reflected the feelings of the local population in saying that the use of the palace for convalescent soldiers had been turned down, but that it was now occupied by a race of people who caused the world horror and disgust. By the end of the month the number of prisoners had reached the thousands. The palace was essentially planned to be used as a transit camp where prisoners arrived and then moved on to the Isle of Man. Many of them came from other camps and from the ships that had been used to house them and then moved on again to other places. Similar to other transit camps, when the number of internees grew so did the likelihood of being a permanent resident.

Until May 1915 there was not a blanket policy of interning all enemy aliens, and the majority of aliens were left alone. The government were still reluctant to implement wholesale civilian internment, especially with a growing number of German military prisoners arriving in the country. Finding accommodation for them all would be a serious challenge. One question that seemed to be unanswered was whether German women would be interned. According to *The Times* it was under consideration at Scotland Yard in mid-May. There was some uncertainty over who should make the decision. The Home Office said that it was a matter for the War Office who in turn claimed that it was a decision that had to be taken by the Home Office. It seemed that neither wanted to make a decision that may have been unpopular, even in the midst of anti-German feeling sweeping the country. German women in London regarded the idea with horror. There was already a shortage of accommodation for men who were interned and would children be interned with mothers? If not what would happen to them. The majority of single women had by this time been repatriated or left the country which meant that those who were left were mainly married women and this would in many cases mean children as well.

The Times made an interesting comment on the situation in which it showed the class consciousness of the times; it said that work for foreign nationals, including women married to Germans, was almost impossible to find, except in the cases of German cooks. Most German servants had been dismissed; one German woman's association said that English women, overwhelmed by the servant difficulty, were still employing German cooks. The absurdity of the situation was shown by a distinguished English archaeologist with a German name; her family had lived in England for more than eighty years, and yet could not obtain work anywhere—this was apparently the norm for anyone with a German name. However, this did not apply if a well-off household was without a cook.

The issue as to which foreign nationals should be interned created yet another problem: recognising who were from enemy countries was not as easy as it seemed. Before the outbreak of war there were a number of different registers of identity, such as the electoral register and lists of National Insurance contributors. None of these gave a complete list of the population and there were few ways of proving a person's nationality. Due to the problem of identifying aliens, there was an attempt to set up a National Registration system. Identity cards were introduced and were given out, after information on the population was compiled by local government. These cards included nationality, which must have been useful for internment purposes, but the real success of the system was that it showed how many men of national service age there were who were still not serving in the forces. Once the system had been used for conscription there was little further interest in it, and the identity cards were virtually forgotten about after the war.

Although the majority of enemy aliens had still not been interned by early May, there were still restrictions on them, and everyone under observation was required to be at home between 9 p.m. and 5 a.m. unless they had a permit. There were also areas near the coast and military complexes that were off limits to aliens. While the government may have been reluctant to persecute those they saw as harmless, certain sections of the public were not. The London Royal Exchange excluded people of German birth, and a demonstration was held by London businessmen who marched to Parliament to urge the government to take sterner action against Germans in Britain. This had an effect and there was a debate in Parliament on the subject later. Sir Henry Dalziel was a strong supporter of the demonstrators and called on the government to take strong measures; he argued that public patience was almost exhausted by the government's ineptitude. Lord Charles Beresford argued that when bombing from zeppelins began in earnest, Germans in London would start fires to add to the confusion. The air raids over England were becoming more common and by the end of May a raid reached as far as the London docks. Unfortunately the bombs that the airship dropped hit housing in the crowded east end, rather than the docks that had been the target. There were seven deaths and more than thirty injured. The numbers were not great, but did cause the population of London a sense of fear that they had never experienced in previous conflicts. The spur for wholesale internment is uncertain—be it the militant views of some politicians or an anti-German press—but within days of the debate the public were showing that their patience was exhausted. This became evident after an increasing number of air raids and the sinking of the *Lusitania*.

One police official said that rumours of forty British soldiers burnt in an aeroplane shed in Holland and the crucifixion of Canadian officers by the Germans were the main sparks that began the riots aimed at enemy aliens. There were several attacks on alien-owned shops in London, while in Southend, where there had been a recent zeppelin raid, rioting was so bad that troops stationed in the area had to be called out to regain control—supported by 200 special constables.

Described by Rudolf Rocker, from a German point of view the yellow press did not hesitate to use the sinking of the *Lusitania* to stir up anti-German feeling to fever heat. Horatio Bottomley in the *John Bull* called for a new vendetta—blood revenge against all Germans living in Britain. Rocker said that many innocent people had to suffer because of incitement by people like him. It should be said that not all newspapers were encouraging hatred of Germans. The *East Ham* and *Stratford Express* said of the early attacks in the east end of London that it was unsportsmanlike and was outlandish to the British institution of fair play. This was definitely the case of some local attacks. A butcher, F. G. Langendorf, had his windows broken in his shop in Barking Road—Langendorf had three brothers serving in the British Army.

The disgust of the British public over the sinking of the *Lusitania* was not reflected everywhere. On the *Royal Edward* the German patriots went mad with joy at the news of the sinking of the liner. A few demonstrated their joy to the guards and it led to fights. One of these men was supposedly religious, but went about congratulating his fellow patriots. Rocker was disgusted at this happiness over the ship with women and children on board being sunk. As a result, all prisoners on the *Royal Edward* were punished. Their post was stopped, which was a severe blow, when they were aware of their anti-German riots going on in London and they did not know if their families were safe. Every day new punitive regulations were introduced, which made everyone miserable. Those on the *Royal Edward* were witness to a number of events in May, such as the zeppelin raids over Southend where a number of people died. They then heard a huge explosion towards the end of the month—the battleship *Princess Irene* blew up in Sheerness, killing hundreds of men on board.

The discussion on the rioting in the House of Commons was not helped when one politician described the riots as expressing the righteous indignation of the nation. To many this seemed to give the violence official endorsement, which also gave the police a reason for not pursuing the miscreants too energetically.

The Times reported on anti-German riots on 13 May. They stated that the demonstrations had continued the previous day and were more serious than on the earlier occasions. Outbreaks of violence occurred in all areas of London, the report listed twenty-four different areas where shops belonging to German or Austrians were attacked. This included more than 150 shops in Kentish Town and Camden Town alone. In the east end of London things were so bad that even shops owned by English shopkeepers closed for the day, with their owners hanging Union Jacks outside their premises. Little work seemed to be carried out in the area while the riots were taking place. Perhaps being part of them was more profitable than working. Not only were the contents of the shops looted, but the insides of shops and houses were badly damaged. Larger items such as furniture were taken away on carts.

In Walthamstow a German hairdresser was attacked and his shop was wrecked. The mob stole all the family belongings, including their clothes. The family were given shelter by a neighbour, but fearing for the elderly neighbour's safety the owner of the shop asked to be interned. The police refused to take him and he eventually took refuge in the local workhouse. The hairdresser's wife had lived in England most of her life. As her husband was not interned she was not entitled to an allowance. Her grown up children had to contribute to the keep of her husband in the workhouse and could not then help their mother. The fear of the rioters made her so nervous that she could not even answer the door.

So many were made homeless by the riots that a Friend's Meeting house in north London was opened as a refuge, but not before permission had to be obtained from the chief of police. Women and children occupied the main room with makeshift beds. The men occupied the schoolroom. The German cook who fed them was described as speaking the pure tongue of Canning Town, which showed how British many of these supposedly enemy aliens were. At one point seventy people were living in the building.

A number of police constables were injured in the east end rioting. In other parts of the city the police were powerless to deal with the large mobs and often stood back, doing little about them. The crowds were dispersed in some areas by a charge of mounted constables, but there seems little doubt that in many people's eyes the riots were justified. Some of those involved did face justice of a kind. At Stratford Police Court thirty-eight people appeared charged with taking part in the riots. They were charged with various offences, such as theft and receiving stolen property. One man was seen diving through a broken shop window shouting to the crowd outside to follow him. All of them were given small fines, mainly of 4s or 5s.

The problems in the east end of London were not deterring all Germans from living there. A corporal, Aylot, who had been wounded and sent home from France told the *East Ham* and *Stratford Express* about some German prisoners captured in France. On their way to the rear one of the prisoners asked if they were being sent to England. He then said 'I hope I get sent to Stratford, my parents have a business in Plaistow'. The prisoner went on to explain that he had his own business at Bow, which he wanted to run and when told he would be held until the war ended he said 'that won't be long as we are nearly beaten already'.

One family in the east end received a letter from their father in May. Mr C. Buhler was a baker from Canning Town. He had been arrested and sent to Frith Hill. In his letter he said that he had plenty to eat and drink, but was cold and wet; he told his wife to tell their young child that he had gone on his summer holiday. Buhler was later released as he had two sons in the British Army—one of them was killed in action.

In Manchester there were attempts to do something about the rioting and there were thirteen arrests for disorderly conduct; the police also arrested shopkeepers of premises that had been attacked for their own protection. Over 200 shops were damaged in Liverpool, causing £40,000 worth of damage. This led to the internment of 150 Germans who were arrested for their own safety and sent under military escort to Hawick.

Southend in Essex had been the victim of an air raid by zeppelins and this was what led to serious outbreaks of violence in the town. A number of premises owned by Germans were attacked in Queen's Road. The military were called out to support the police and drove the mob into the High Street, but once there they attacked another shop.

There were other outbreaks of violence in places such as Newcastle; in Cardiff and Glasgow public opinion had turned against Germans and although there were no reports of serious violence there were calls to restrict the rights of enemy aliens. In Nottingham and Bradford naturalised Germans declared their loyalty to Britain and in some cases claimed that their sons were fighting for the country, but this often made little difference to how they were treated. The violence in cities was the most pronounced and aliens living in the countryside may have been less susceptible to rioting, but their position was often worse than those living in cities. At least in a large urban area there was a chance of anonymity. In the countryside everyone would know if a local was a foreigner. Because of the rioting there was a hastily summoned meeting of the cabinet, but no firm decision about mass internment was made; the government felt that enough had been done to protect the country from enemy aliens and that any further action taken would have to be to protect enemy aliens from the country. This calm reaction was because the government still had no reason to suspect that the majority of the aliens in the country were in any way a danger. Whether the opposition, who were calling for widespread internment, actually believed that what they were asking for was necessary, or if it was just an attempt to gain public support, is another matter. As such, many government agencies were interested in the process of internment and a committee was formed with members from several different departments. This committee was responsible for opening a number of new camps, but the majority of early internees still ended up in the Isle of Man at Knockaloe Camp. This was the second camp set up on the Isle of Man and had previously been a Territorial Army base.

Despite the government's fairly relaxed attitude, there were of course many people whose resulting incarceration seems to have been rather harsh, if not ridiculous. However, deciding who was to be arrested and who wasn't must have been a very hard decision to make and there was always the worry of what would happen to enemy aliens who were left free. The government's rules were overseen by public officials, and tended to be interpreted very rigidly often leading to mistakes.

What really seemed to turn widespread public opinion against enemy aliens was the beginning of all-out U-boat war by the Germans, especially after the sinking of the *Lusitania* that had taken place on 7 May 1915, with nearly 1,200 civilian deaths, including over 100 children. Bombing by zeppelins also had an effect. There were also numerous rumours of atrocities carried out by German troops. All of these events had been rigorously reported in some sections of the press with added calls for revenge.

The Manchester Guardian published a speech by Mr Asquith who said that 'no one could be surprised at the progressive violation by the enemy of civilised warfare and the rules of humanity'. This had aroused feelings of righteous indignation in all classes. He went on to say that it was the innocent and unoffending persons who are made to pay for the crimes of others. There seemed to be a conflict of meaning in his speech, by stating that the indignation was righteous could have been interpreted as permission to persecute aliens by those looking for approval. Although, saying that it was the innocent and unoffending who suffered seemed to be a support for the aliens who were the ones suffering. He further stated that from a military point of view that the internment, so far carried out, had provided the safety of the country. The recent events and feelings in the country have made it necessary to look beyond military considerations and the government would consider internment on a more comprehensive scale. It would seem that the press-inspired rioting was what was formulating government policy.

The stories told by survivors helped to turn the horror of the *Lusitania* disaster into reality. Alice Drury was eighteen and had been employed as a nurse to the two children of an American couple. She was below decks when the torpedo struck and struggled to take the two children up onto the deck—one of which was a young baby. She spent twelve hours in a lifeboat with the children before they were rescued; many other women and children were not so lucky. There were no men in the lifeboat.

A petition was presented to the government by Mr Joynson-Hicks, signed by a quarter-of-a-million women, who asked for the internment of all aliens of a military age to protect their homes. In Mr Joynson-Hicks view there seemed to be no innocent aliens. It was eventually decided by Asquith that civilians from enemy countries would be interned for their own safety. This decision might have been influenced by the fact that some of those who had already been interned did not help the cause of their countrymen, but played into the hands of those who were shouting loudest for internment to take place.

Acting as though they were opposed to Britain is understandable, given the resentment they must have felt at being locked up, but certain incidents created problems. For example, internees on the Isle of Man had regularly been taken for walks along country roads in groups of 200. This went on until they cheered the sinking of the *Lusitania*, not an action designed to convince the public that the interned men were really loyal subjects of Britain.

Rudolf Rocker commented on the feelings of German patriotism that grew amongst internees when he was in the camp at Olympia. He said that many of the men were almost hysterical in their patriotism; it was the last thing he expected from Germans abroad. However, most of these men had been law-abiding citizens of England for many years; they were then hunted by mobs, their homes destroyed, and then they were arrested and flung into prison. They were being punished for being German, so they had to justify themselves as Germans.

The Times reported on 14 May that the government had at last decided to do what they should have done nine months before. They were, in the reporters words, 'to make a clean sweep of enemy aliens'. This was not quite true as the report went on to explain. Asquith had told the Commons that there were 19,000 aliens already interned, with 40,000 still at large. Numbers seemed to vary in other reports. Of these, 24,000 were men. The plan was that all men of military age would be interned. Older men were to be sent back to Germany, along with some women and children. He went on to explain that those who had been naturalised, thought to be around 8,000, were British citizens, but of hostile origin—these would also be interned if it was seen to be necessary.

There has always been a view that the government were forced into interning large numbers of aliens for their own protection and that it was due to public pressure. This was not the case according to Paul Cohen-Portheim. He said that the camps on the Isle of Man had been under construction for some time before large-scale internment began and so it must have been the government's aim all along. If Cohen-Portheim's view is correct then perhaps it was seen that large-scale internment was seen as inevitable by the government, and the delay was a way of getting enough camps ready before it finally happened.

The decisions as to who would be interned were to be made by an advisory body. It would have the power to exempt some from internment. There was some disquiet in *The Times* report as to some of those who had already been interned and later released. There was a feeling that exemptions may have been decided on the person's social status. There was a danger that the richer the alien the more chance of him being excused internment. This was while the report went on to claim that the poor aliens were not the most dangerous.

It was later stated that the committee would report to the Home Secretary and it would be his decision as to whether a person was excused. As for naturalised aliens, it would be for the committee to decide if they posed a threat or not. Bonor Law endorsed the new proposals and stated that this was not a war between armies, but between nations and those who are not with us are against us.

The news of the government plans seemed to put an end to the worst of the rioting, although the wet weather at the time may have also helped. That and the fact that there was a severe shortage of bread in the east end of London, due to attacks on bakers. Despite a decline in violence, the new plans on internment did not stop a meeting at the Mansion House—presided over by the Mayor of London—of women against the continued freedom of aliens in the country. During the comparative peace following the riots, there were attempts by the police to recover some of the stolen property. In the east end of London much of the contraband was being sold at very cheap rates. There were reports of a piano being sold for half a crown. A great deal of stolen items were recovered, especially in relation to furniture. There were a few examples of further attacks in the east end of London still taking place, but they seem to have been more aimed at gain or excitement than in attacks on enemy aliens. In Custom House, jeweller's shops were attacked and robbed. A nearby public house was then attacked and the landlord came out and offered anyone in the mob £1,000 if they could prove he was not a born Englishman. A drapery shop in Barking Road was robbed, but the owner was clearly an Englishman.

The same thing occurred in Leytonstone where shops were attacked and robbed whatever the nationality of their proprietors. As well as trying to find stolen property, the police in London were ordered by the Commissioner of Police to arrest all aliens of military age in all the divisions under his control. The police were told to warn the men that they would be arrested the next day, but whether this actually happened in most cases is debatable.

By the end of May, both the *Royal Edward* and the *Saxonia* were discontinued as internment camps. When the men were taken off the ships they walked off the end of Southend Pier to be met by a sullen crowd of locals who watched them pass. Rudolf Rocker said that they watched them angrily, but there were no attempts at attacks. Many of the men were sent to Alexandra Palace. The move towards wholesale internment led to the creation of new camps almost immediately. On 4 June, *The Manchester Guardian* reported that Clapham Common, which had been taken over by the War Office for military use, was being surrounded by a barbed wire fence for use as an internment camp.

As internment spread, a detective finally arrived to arrest Paul Cohen-Portheim who had still been working as a costume designer. An alien still working at this time was a rarity. He was told to pack as though he was going on holiday and was informed that he was going to Stratford and thought it would be pleasant to be in the place of Shakespeare's birth. Instead he was taken to an old factory in Stratford, east London, with a broken glass roof. Soldiers at the camp took his sketch books, which he never saw again. After a few days some of the men, including Cohen-Portheim, were taken from this clearing station and were marched through the streets to the railway station. By this time public opinion had hardened against them. The streets were lined with crowds, many of whom were hostile and who called them baby killers. Another alien taken to Stratford was Richard Notschke. He wrote a description of the rioting in east London in May. He said that it started as if at a signal and in one night over a 1,000 German shops and homes were destroyed. The authorities seemed powerless to stop it or did not want to interfere. When Notschke was interned he was sent to Stratford and was stood in a small courtyard. The soldiers guarding the camp pushed the new arrivals around and searched their luggage. While they stood in the rain, anything of value and any money over £1 was taken from them by the guards.

Despite claims that no mistreatment of aliens took place in Britain's camps Notschke said that a sergeant major went round punching men in the neck so that their hats would fall off and he could see that they were hiding nothing. The officer in charge did nothing to stop this. Although the camp was supposedly only a transit site, Notshke said that many men had been there up to a year and it was to stay open for many more years.

Although Cohen–Portheim had previously said that there was little animosity shown against him, this had changed in many areas. The crowds watching the internees marching to the station at Stratford threw things at them and called them baby killers, a name given to the men operating the airships now bombing the country and this was common elsewhere. The journey to the Isle of Man was a strange one for Cohen-Portheim, he had expected to be moved in a cattle truck, but found himself on a normal passenger train where lunch was served to them. The journey on a steamer from Liverpool was very different when they were locked below decks until they arrived at the Isle of Man. There were a number of men moved from Stratford in June. There were at least two groups moved during the month, with 500 internees in each. When one group was walking to the station, a young man fell behind and stepped onto the pavement. He was dragged off by a soldier and then forcibly marched to the station by a policeman. The groups had armed escorts and were described as mainly young men.

Cohen-Portheim was taken to Knockaloe Camp and found that it wasn't finished—there were no wash houses, chairs, or beds. The inmates were of various classes, many were sailors taken off ships. They developed into two classes, those with money who could draw £1 a week to spend (about 10 per cent of the inmates) and the rest who tried to work and earn money from those who had it. An internment camp had been established early in the war at Douglas on the Isle of Man. It was here that many of the new internees were taken. The later Knockaloe camp consisted of five compounds, holding about 1,000 men in each compound. There was a canteen outside the fence with a window opening into the camp, but huge queues built up and the canteen soon sold out of goods. Although originally planned for 5,000 internees, the camp grew as the war carried on and eventually held around 23,000 internees in twenty-three compounds. Other camps were also later constructed on the island.

At Alexandra Palace, Rudolf Rocker was not happy. He thought that the commandant Lieutenant Colonel R. S. Frowd Walker was too much of a military man to understand civilian prisoners. There were some advantages though; counting of the prisoners took place inside after breakfast, not on the cold windy deck of a ship. There was also an area outside where they could go for exercise. The relief of being counted inside on Rocker's first day was not repeated as they later had to stand for hours outside in the compound in the hot sun being counted again. The counting took place three times a day and during this some of the older men fainted in the hot sun. At night there were always three armed sentries in the great hall who marched up and down keeping everyone awake. There was also stamping and presenting of arms and the shouting of orders when the sentries were changed. Visitors were allowed, but had to sit across a table with a partition in the centre to stop them touching. Rocker was responsible for having some of the restrictions lifted, such as the no touching rule for visitors and the sentries making a noise at nights. He said that the commandant could be very reasonable when he was feeling well. At other times, when he felt sick, he was much stricter—the man was very ill and so was often not reasonable. This was a clear example of how the commandant of each camp was responsible for how the internees lived.

As well as civilian aliens being interned, another German was being held in the Tower of London. Carl Frederick Muller had landed at Sunderland in January claiming to be a Russian. He sent a large quantity of letters to Rotterdam, as well as visiting the city on a number of occasions. He had also recruited a baker to help him—both men were eventually arrested.

Although many of those arrested on suspicion of spying early in the war were just interned, Muller and his accomplice went to trial. At the trial at the Old Bailey the baker was imprisoned, while Muller was sentenced to death and was shot on 23 June in the tower. Messages were still sent in his name giving bogus details and Muller was awarded the Iron Cross and sent £400 from Germany after his death. He was later dismissed as the bogus details of his information became clear to his masters.

The sudden increase in the number of internees led to camps springing up in many places, some of which were entirely unsuitable. Internment camps presented different problems to what POW camps did. Military prisoners were used to camp life and to discipline. The first POW camps were mainly set up in the west and the north, away from ports near to the continent. German military prisoners seemed less upset about finding themselves in captivity. In many cases they found the safety and relative comfort of the camps a relief after the discomfort and horror of the trenches—boredom is easier to bear if the alternative is being shot. Some of the first internment camps were terrible, especially for those who had been living in middle-class comfort. One, in an old factory at Queensferry, was dirty and the roof leaked. There were no beds and the inmates petitioned the Foreign Office to try and get improvements. At the camp at Dorchester there were three baths for 1,200 inmates. Strangely, the government saw one of the biggest problems in the early camps was that all classes were held together in the same camps.

There were also claims of mistreatment at some camps. At Woking there was said to be a cell with no heating, that was too small to allow a man to lie down, and that had no glass in the window; it was used as a punishment for prisoners. At Brockton camp in Staffordshire the commandant had been himself a prisoner in a German camp and so hated Germans. Even wounded men on crutches were made to scrub the floors and he would stop the prisoner's coal supply on a whim.

The constant claims of mistreatment from both sides can perhaps be explained by a report from the Society of Friends. They stated that the people of every country were taught by their governments to believe that they treated POWs, either civilian or military, with the greatest humanity, while their enemies treated their prisoners with the utmost cruelty. This was shown by an American YMCA worker who had visited camps for Russian prisoners in Germany. He had prepared a booklet showing the best of the conditions in the camps. He then went to Russia and met the Russian Minister of War and showed him the booklet. The Russian General ordered the booklets to be destroyed; he told the American that he did not want their people to know about good treatment of prisoners by the Germans. There is little doubt that this idea also applied to England. The Society of Friends often visited camps in Germany and then sent reports on how well many of the prisoners were being treated to the British press. The majority of the newspapers were not interested in publishing the stories. The only exceptions were *The Manchester Guardian* and the *Westminster Gazette*. Not only did most of the English newspapers refuse to publish these stories, but the *Evening News* called the Society Hun Coddlers and claimed that they supplied food and luxuries to interned prisoners. They were not permitted to do this and had never tried to do so.

'There was a lot of interest in the press regarding the increase in internment after the government's change of heart. There were reports of many surrendering themselves before they could be arrested. Public attitude also seemed to have softened towards the aliens. The feeling against aliens in the Baltic Exchange was said to have become less extreme, especially after many naturalised Germans signed a declaration of their anger at German barbarities. One of those who signed was a Mr J. Hess who had been living in London for sixty-six years. His son had been a lieutenant in the Royal Horse Artillery and had been killed at Ypres. Another one who signed was Mr J. C. M. Friedberger who had been a stockbroker in England since 1875 and had two sons and a grandson in the British Army and another son in the National Guard, as well as a grandson in the Navy.

The spread of internment was mainly a civilised affair, with many of those to be interned going to police stations with their belongings and handing themselves in. Many seemed pleased to do so, perhaps finally accepting what they had been under the threat of for so long. Others were those who had lost their businesses or jobs and were destitute with no means of support. Far from being happy at the voluntary surrender of so many aliens, the authorities suddenly found themselves overwhelmed with nowhere to put the new arrivals. The camps already in existence were mainly full and there were no new ones ready for them. Most of the thousands newly interned in London were sent to Stratford or Southend. The provision of new camps was still the responsibility of the military.

A special train left Fenchurch Street on for Southend carrying 150 internees as well as normal passengers. Police and soldiers were waiting at Southend Station. They were described as a crowd of decently dressed men who might have been leaving on a day trip to the seaside. There was some debate over this as it was only a military matter if they were being interned because they were of a military danger to the state. If they were being interned for their own safety then it would make them a civil problem. Whoever was responsible, it was clear that there were not enough camps or guards for the numbers to be interned, which was why there had been no great rush to carry out the new regulations. More than a 1,000 aliens had arrived at Frimley in the few days since widespread internment had begun. They were carried on special trains from Waterloo and then marched to Frith Hill. One crowd marched from the station into captivity singing 'Tipperary' to show where their loyalties lay.

The situation was different in some parts of London. Although many of the better off aliens had put their affairs in order and volunteered for internment in the east end, there were many who were not so keen to comply. There were 400 arrests in the east end where many of the young aliens of German and Austrian extraction were claiming to be Russian. This was hard to disprove in areas where large settlements of aliens lived.

There was a danger of the situation getting out of hand as the police had to slow the process of arresting men of military age with nowhere to send them. As well as the men, there were problems with large numbers of women and children who were presenting themselves to the Emergency Committee for the Assistance of Germans, Austrians and Hungarians in distress. This was based at St Stephen's House Westminster. Many of the women were British born with German husbands. Some were homeless due to anti-alien rioting. Many had lost their breadwinner who had been interned. Some were given food and lodging at a building that was under police protection.

It was not only enemy aliens who were the target of an anti-German press. Lord Haldene, the Lord Chancellor, had been the target of the *Daily Express* for some years. He was criticised for being pro-German and like many of the upper classes he did have strong German connections. He had been educated in Germany, but other claims made about him were ridiculous. He was accused of being the illegitimate son of the Kaiser and also criticised as he had a dog named Kaiser. Eventually he was forced to resign from the government.

In a great piece of propaganda, the Bryce Committee published the 'Report of the Committee on Alleged German Outrages' soon after the sinking of the *Lusitania*. The committee chairman was Viscount James Bryce. The report was timed to appear just after the *Lusitania* outrage as it would then have a greater effect and contained details of the supposed atrocities that took place after the invasion of Belgium by the Germans. Most of the claims included in the report of the widespread slaughter of Belgian civilians, including women and children, were unsubstantiated. The Belgian government had asked that the witnesses to these events were not to be named due to the danger of reprisals against their families. There were counter claims by the Germans that Belgian civilians were operating as guerrillas and that they were responsible for atrocities against German soldiers, including torturing the wounded. The report was accepted by a world, which seemed eager to believe the worst of the Germans. It was circulated in most

European countries and was widely read in America, including being published in numerous American newspapers. It is thought that the report may have had some effect on the Americans eventually entering the war.

There is little doubt that the Belgian government pushed hard for the support of the Allies after the German invasion. As early as September, 1914, a Belgian mission (including Belgian Minister of Justice M. Carlton de Wiart and a number of ministers of state) appeared in a meeting with the Eighty Club (which included many politicians) at the Hotel Cecil in London. The mission was there to make claims of German atrocities in their country to gain support. They were then due to travel to America for the same reason. The belief of German atrocities taking place suited both the Belgians and the British as a means of turning the rest of the world against the Germans and the report is now seen as a work of propaganda rather than one based on facts. Just before the report was published, the Germans brought out what was known as the *White Book*. It was a means of combatting the expected criticism of the Bryce report. In it there were claims that the reason why so many Belgian civilians died was because many of them were acting as an armed resistance who often fired on the German troops, and were responsible for attacking and maiming wounded German soldiers.

The German argument was that the attacks by civilians did not conform to the generally recognised rules of international law. They claimed that in an organised people's war, the people may be recognised as a militia or volunteer corps only if they wore a badge, openly bear weapons, and have a responsible leader. The argument that Belgium resistance was illegal seemed to ignore the fact that Germany had acted illegally in invading neutral Belgium. The content of the German *White Book* was included in the book, written by J. H. Morgan, *German Atrocities* (published in 1916). Morgan had been involved in the Bryce report and his book included material that had not been included in it. The popularity of the subject was shown by the fact that the book was reprinted ten times in the year it was published.

It is not clear how much German soldiers knew about what was going on in England. There is little doubt that the German press were often accusing the British of mistreating POWs and they also mentioned the difficulties being suffered by German civilians in Britain. This could have had an effect in how the German soldiers saw the English. The same could be true of the British soldiers. The *Daily*

Mail was widely distributed amongst the troops in France who must have been influenced by its anti-German views. These claims of British mistreatment of prisoners could have been a reason for the poor treatment of prisoners in German captivity, but could also have had an effect on treatment of the English on the battlefield. There were claims of British wounded soldiers being left in a trench who were later found with their throats cut. A German officer of the 13 Regiment of the 13 Division of the VII German Corps left a diary stating that the sight of his men beating British wounded to death affected him so deeply.

In June Friedrich Schmidt was shot and killed while trying to escape from the camp at Leigh. This seems to have been a very isolated incident. His funeral was attended by large crowds of locals and fourteen of his comrades from the camp were also allowed to be there. Later funerals, for those who died in the camp from natural causes (some from the influenza outbreak later in the war), were all very well attended.

The arrests of those involved in anti-German rioting were beginning to be dealt with in courts by June. At Manchester City Police Court there were seventeen defendants, eight women and nine men charged with stealing or receiving stolen goods belonging to Leonard Lambert, a pork butcher of Stanley Street Openshaw. Lambert was of German birth, but was a naturalised English citizen. In May, his home was attacked by a large crowd and furniture, including beds and birdcages, were taken away. His home was then set on fire and damage was also caused to other houses owned by him, to the value of £800. The crowd numbered around 1,000.

The seventeen people in court all claimed that the stolen items found in their possession had been given to them or were found on the streets. The chairman of the bench said that the defendants no doubt had strong feelings on certain matters as he had himself. He did not express them by stealing bird cages. He was satisfied that since the incident the defendants regretted their conduct. Therefore the defendants were discharged, except in some cases; the exceptions were five of the defendants who were fined a very lenient 5s or 10s.

The number of men arriving in the Isle of Man was growing by this time. One report on those who arrived at the camps described them as a motley crew, but they came from all walks of life. It was said that one of them could have a cheque for seven figures honoured anywhere in Britain, while others could not get credit for a glass of beer. Many of the inmates had been well-regarded and wealthy men, which seemed to disprove the rumour that the wealthiest aliens did not get interned. They soon discovered that in the camp there was no hierarchy, and the rules of life on the outside did not apply at first in the camps. A new word, *schiebung*, was coined—meaning an act by which one gained an illegitimate advantage. It was a way of the men achieving some level of success. Although the men had been allowed to bring their belongings with them they had nowhere to put them. The average hut's furniture consisted of a table and mattresses. When Cohen-Portheim managed to obtain two nails to hang things on he described them as the greatest acquisition of his life. It showed how small events meant so much to the men interned.

The camps were gradually organised and hut captains were elected. Letters could be written twice a week, but to get past the censors they had to contain no mention of the war or conditions in the camp. A camp bank was set up and those with money could draw £1 a week. There then developed two classes: the moneyed class, which totalled about 10 per cent of the inmates, and the other 90 per cent, who tried to make money as barbers, valets, and shoe shiners. It was even possible to pay someone to take your place at the weekly chore of potato peeling. Although supposedly interned for their own safety, the new arrivals were told by their commandant that during any attempt at escape they would be warned once and then shot. It seems they had more to fear from the guards than from the public outside the camp. New regulations were introduced during the war so that prisoners of war, including internees, could be tried by military rather than civilian courts. The lieutenant governor of the Isle of Man was given the authority to hold these courts, and over 300 prisoners on the island were at one time or another tried, sentenced, and transferred to the prison at Douglas, and then to the mainland. The charge against many was attempting to escape.

Problems inside the camps were not always due to the treatment by the guards. In Alexandra Place, Rudolf Rocker had obtained permission from the commandant to hold a number of lectures in the theatre. Rocker had agreed that these would be about German literature. The patriotic Germans in the camp complained to the commandant because he was an anarchist. The lectures were cancelled because the claimed they could cause trouble in the camp. The cancellation did then cause trouble as the majority of the prisoners wanted them to go ahead. The men who had complained were now faced by a hostile majority and asked Rocker to calm things down. They had obviously not expected such a reaction and then petitioned the governor to let the lectures take place. Lectures by members of the camps inmates were not the only ones to take place. There were a number of religious organisations who visited the camp, including the Bishop of London who said that god had sent the war as a punishment for their sins. I'm not sure if he only meant German sins or those of all races. Religious publications also often arrived, some from Germany. One warned the men against sexual perversions, though there was little chance of this happening as there was never any privacy in the camp.

The anti-German feeling that had washed across the country in May had been encouraged by some areas of the press. One of the most vociferous in its hatred of enemy aliens was the *John Bull*. The increase in internment was obviously still not good enough for them and they wanted to take the persecution of aliens even further. The magazine had published a request for people to join the Anti-German Pledge. The pledge included promises not to employ aliens, not to buy anything made by aliens, to have no social intercourse with them, and to ostracise from respectable society any woman who marries a German. The editor of the newspaper was Horatio Bottomley MP who was one of the strongest anti-alien members of Parliament.

The end of May saw the first air raid to take place over London. One of those to experience the raid was Sylvia Pankhurst who was present as a welfare worker in the east end. The raid caused seven deaths and thirty-five injuries. Miss Pankhurst described the terror the raid caused, but also described the result of the attack, which was to attract numerous people who wanted to see the results of the raid. Pankhurst said that the following day the east end was full of well-dressed people in cars who had come to see the effects of the air raid. There were also photographers, military officers, Red Cross nurses, and people who had travelled from miles away to see what had happened. A rumour that Shoreditch Church had been damaged led to crowds gathering around it, but this proved to be false. Most of the damage had been in Hoxton and in one house, where a child had been killed, a soldier on duty at the door had trouble holding back the crowds, despite the fact that the house was still being occupied by the child's family. There were rumours that lights had been shown to enable the enemy to drop their bombs, the blame would be placed on any aliens in the area. Someone lighting a cigarette in the dark was liable to be attacked as a German spy. There were more anti-German riots when it was believed that it was German residents who had carried out the signalling. Miss Pankhurst witnessed a woman being attacked by a mob until she was on the ground being kicked by them. She asked a nearby soldier to help and he refused to interfere. An officer in a car was passing and she asked him to help, but was told he was too busy on Army business. Eventually the police arrived and stopped the assault. The attack had been carried out by the *LZ.38*, commanded by Major Linnarz. The airship dropped 119 bombs over Leytonstone, Stoke Newington, Whitechapel, Stepney, and Shoreditch. Linnarz later said that he imagined that he could hear faint cries of tortured souls as he released the bombs so there must have been some feelings of guilt over his actions.

The Isle of Man camps had a hospital, with one doctor per camp and it was run by orderlies with first aid experience. If the doctor did not speak German and the patient did not speak English then the patients could spend quite some time there. The orderlies often charged the sick for everything, and rumour has it they did their best to keep a well-off patient in hospital as long as possible. Previously undiscovered illnesses were being observed and named as the war progressed—not just shell shock, which occurred among soldiers at the front, but also barbed wire sickness, which was observed in the camps and included all the mental health symptoms caused by confinement.

It appears that there were a number of people in the camps who should not have been there at all, as they were not enemy aliens. Lack of a strict identification system was often the cause of this. Cohen-Portheim described a number of these men interned with him. They included a Mexican seaman whose mother did not know what his father's name was and had named him Shultz. This German name was enough of a reason for him to be taken off his ship and interned. There was an Egyptian who had described himself as faithful to the Caliph (meaning his religion) and had therefore been interned as a Turk. There was even an English boy who had gone to live in Australia with his parents. He returned to Europe, arriving in England as war broke out. Being interested in architecture, he was drawing some attractive buildings when he was arrested as a spy—the buildings turned out to be defences. As he had no papers proving his nationality he was interned.

Although the Douglas holiday camp was used to house internees in the war, for its inmates it must have been far from a holiday. They were guarded by the Isle of Man Volunteers, later reinforced by the Royal

Defence Corps. The internees mainly slept in tents at the beginning, but had more permanent dining halls. There were three different sections in this camp, the privileged or gentlemen's camp (in which prisoners paid for the privilege of being interned in a better class of prison), the Jewish camp, and the ordinary camp for everyone else. Although most camps were much the same, there were two that were known as gentlemen's camps, the one at Douglas and at Wakefield. The latter, Lofthouse Park, was rumoured to be a large country house where every internee had their own room and the freedom of the large gardens, but the truth was very different. Although Lofthouse Park had indeed been a stately home, conditions for internees were not grand as the house itself was occupied by the commandant. The grounds housed three camps, each holding 500 men. The major difference from other camps was that inmates could buy numerous items, such as furniture, while the canteen was also much better supplied than other camps—even alcohol was available. Inmates could draw up to £3 a week from the bank, and had to pay 10s a week to stay in the camp. It seems ludicrous that men had to pay to be interned, but this was accepted by those with money in return for better conditions. To combat the boredom suffered by internees at Lofthouse Park there were lectures organised, covering topics such as history, science, and foreign languages. In fact anyone who had anything interesting to talk about could give a lecture. There were also musical recitals and a camp orchestra was formed. Many of those interned were musicians and academics. The conditions for German prisoners of war in English camps were, it seems, quite good. The food given to prisoners was probably of the same—if not better—quality that working men would have been used to. Money and food could also be sent to the prisoners from Germany.

There are so many reports of brutality and bad treatment in German camps that there would seem to be some element of truth in them. The National Archives contain numerous interviews with British prisoners of the Germans during the First World War, and many contain stories of incredible brutality, even including the murder of prisoners—a crime that often went unpunished. An interview with Private Arthur Soder of the Dorset Regiment is a good example. Private Soder was one of a group of 1,000 British prisoners who were sent to work on the frontline in Russia, in retaliation for German prisoners being forced to work on the docks at Le Havre. Retaliation was often the excuse given for poor treatment. He tells of continuous beatings by the guards who used their rifle butts. A common punishment was being tied to a pole while standing on a box. The box was then kicked away, leaving the prisoner hanging off the ground. This happened for a number of hours, several days at a time. The men were also forced to work on the frontline trenches while under fire from the Russians. They suffered from severe frostbite, to the extent that many men lost their toes, but still had to work every day. At one camp in Larchen a private from the Coldstream Guards was shot dead by a guard because he could not walk. Although there was an enquiry nothing happened to the guard who continued to work with prisoners.

Another report was from Private Brooks, a member of the 23rd Service Battalion Royal Fusiliers. This was the famous Sportsman's Battalion, which consisted of men from the world of entertainment who were allowed to join the battalion up to the age of forty-five, the normal limit for enlistment to the ranks was thirty-five. Private Brooks was captured by the Germans. He reported that the prisoners were forced to eat boiled nettles and dandelions, while a small loaf of bread had to be shared between five men when it was available, which was rarely. There was often twenty-two hours between meals, despite the men being engaged full time in heavy manual work. Although treated well at first, this changed when Brooks reached Phalemphin. This was in France and is correct as written in Brook's account. It was not unusual for a guard to rush into a group of British prisoners and punch one of them in the face for no reason. This was followed by tying the prisoners to a tree, forcing them to stoop for hours. On Brooks' release he found that one of his friends was said to have died of wounds while in captivity. He said that he had seen the man after his capture, and he had not been wounded then.

However, not all the German camps were as bad as this. Ruhleben camp, near Berlin, in Germany was used for civilian internees and was inspected by a Dane, Mr A. Goudsmit. He described the condition of the prisoners as very satisfactory, having inspected the food, sanitary arrangements, and heating. Most of the men had beds and there was a canteen that sold food. Concerts were put on and the money raised by an admission charge of a penny was distributed to the poorer prisoners in the camp. The camp was once a trotting track and held about 4,000 British prisoners. They were of all ages, social class, and conditions of health. They were at first lodged in stables and the grandstand, some even lived in horse boxes, but the camp improved enormously later in the war after new barracks were built. This did not stop the British press from criticising conditions at the camp. It was often said that British civilians in Germany were living in poor conditions. This was often written in the newspapers that were most critical of Germans.

It is clear that British servicemen were not always above reproach in their treatment of German prisoners. There are many reports of German prisoners being bayoneted after capture because they would not come back to the British trenches. A letter from the commanding officer of the Ulster Division reports that they took more prisoners than other units because they were more kind-hearted. I take this meant that they took their prisoners back rather than killed them. There were even reports that German troops were told that the British kept black soldiers behind the lines to kill prisoners, as the frontline troops would not do it.

In Britain, however, the situation regarding prisoners' confinement seems to have been more open than in Germany. The inspector of British Camps was the former US Minister to Cuba and Rumania, J. B. Jackson. He was allowed to inspect any camp without making an appointment, and was permitted to speak to prisoners alone. His comments about Frith Hill Camp in Aldershot state that the prisoners ran a 'little republic' under their own NCOs, and that they had their own police force. There was no work for the prisoners, but they said that they were treated with respect by the camp guards. The food was the same as that supplied to the British Army, with the rations actually coming from the Aldershot Army Service Corps stores.

The press interest in internment tailed off slightly after the first flush of the arrest of so many aliens. In June, however, *The Times* turned its attention to those who were claiming exemption from arrest, rather than those who were interned. The judicial body to decide on exemption met daily in Westminster Hall. There were two committees, one for England and Ireland and one for Scotland. The committees consisted of two members of Parliament and a judge from the High Court. To apply for exemption, applicants had to send in a form obtainable from the Home Office containing details of birth, occupation, and the reason for exemption. There had been more than 2,000 applications by this time; 286 were successful, 600 needed further investigation, and 1,256 were refused outright. There were also applications for exemption from repatriation. These were often from British born women who were married to aliens. There had been no decision on these cases as yet.

There were several agreements made between Germany and Britain regarding wounded prisoners. One of these was arranged through the

Dutch, and involved sending home many men from both sides that had lost limbs or were hopeless invalids and would never be able to fight again. It was even suggested that all prisoners should be released after two years in captivity, but the Germans didn't reply to this British offer. When prisoners were taken in France they were treated very well by the British Army, being well fed and housed—this was witnessed by neutral observers as well as the British.

There was an escape at Shrewsbury Camp in June when Bernhardt Johannes Zimpell, a member of a Prussian Regiment, and Otto Ricart Kircner managed to get out of the camp. They succeeded in covering around 20 miles before being recaptured close to Welshpool. They were apprehended by Captain Dugdale of the Montgomeryshire Yeomanry and Captain R. Williams of the Welsh Guards. The two officers had been driving to Welshpool and had heard of the escape when they came across the two prisoners. They were returned to the camp. In 1915 two Germans escaped from Donington Hall; a reward of £100 was offered for information on Lieutenants Thelen and Keilback. They were recaptured in the Chatham area a few days after escaping. In July 1915 a tunnel was discovered at Leigh camp and the three ringleaders of the escape plot were sent to Woking Prison for three months' hard labour. Escape from some camps did not seem very difficult. When Rudolf Rocker thought about escaping from Alexandra Palace he found that another young prisoner had also considered it. Rocker needed to get a message to his friends outside to see if they could hide him if he escaped. The young man, August Arndt, agreed to escape and carry the message. He would do so and get back before he was missed. Arndt had found some loose boards that gave access to the underground railway station, which had served the Palace before it closed. He left the camp at 10 p.m., but did not return in the morning. For the first day the men covered him by moving someone who had already been counted to be counted twice. Eventually his absence was noticed and all inmates were confined to their quarters. Visits and letters were also stopped for all the internees.

Following this punishment, the men complained to commandant that they were unhappy at being treated like soldiers and not civilians—punishing all of them for what one man had done. The commandant responded by telling the inmates that government orders were to treat them like that, due to the majority of them having had military experience. However, he was surprised to find this information false and cancelled all punishments.

Ardnt was captured the following day. He had got lost trying to find Rocker's home and was so late that he could not get back to the camp the next day. When he did return he heard the alarm so got out again, and after another failed attempt to re-enter the camp he found that his escape route had been blocked. He then hung around outside until he was seen and recaptured. Ardnt was court martialled. He did not reveal Rocker's part in the escape, but said he had wanted some time to himself as his mother was sick and two of his brothers were missing in the war. He was sentenced to 168 days hard labour and served his sentence in a prison.

In July there was a multiple escape from Alexandra Palace. This was an unusual, but not entirely unexpected event, although most escapees were from military camps while this was a civilian internment camp. The three men named Duber, Seyssert, and Stauffer were recaptured at Coles Grove, Hertfordshire—8 miles from the camp. They were finally found in a garden shed by the gardener on the property of Mr H. Raincock. They had only been free for a few hours and were returned to the camp. Although there were many escape attempts from camps in Britain, an unusual event occurred in July in which a prisoner escaped and managed to get back to Germany—the only one to achieve this throughout the war. Gunther Plüschow was a naval flying officer who had been in China at the outbreak of the war. He had managed to get away to America and then, while trying to get to Germany, he was captured in Gibraltar and sent to England where he was eventually held in Donington Hall. Plüschow claimed that he was plotting escape from the moment he arrived at the camp and, with another officer, he reported sick so that he would not be missed at roll call and during a heavy storm they hid in the grounds. The two men prepared as best they could, but had no papers and identity cards that had just been introduced to Britain. They climbed the wire, despite part of it being electrified and having large spikes on it and then they walked to Derby. From there, the two men split up and Plüschow took a train to Leicester and then one to London. The officer he had escaped with, Trefftz, was supposed to meet him at St Paul's Cathedral, but never showed up. After spending the night in a garden he went into Hyde Park and slept on a bench. He later saw a poster that told him that his friend had been recaptured. Plüschow disguised himself by using Vaseline, coal dust, and boot polish to dye his hair black. He said that he looked like a sailor and no one would have suspected him of being an officer. An advantage perhaps given by the class system in the country at the time. While on a bus, he heard two men discussing a Dutch steamer about to leave from Tilbury that afternoon.

After travelling to Tilbury by train he spotted the Dutch ship the *Mecklenburg* tied up at a buoy. He crossed the river to Gravesend and planned to swim out to the ship and stow away, though he became trapped in deep mud and missed the boat. He had to wait a few days before he got the chance to climb aboard the steamer *Princess Juliana* and hid in one of the lifeboats. Once the boat arrived in Flushing, Plüschow climbed out onto the deck and no one took any notice of him. He managed to get off the ship and took a train to Germany.

Herman Tholens had been the second in command of a German U-boat, the *Mainz,* and was captured at Heligoland in August 1914 when the submarine was sunk. He spent an hour in the sea before being picked up by a British Destroyer. He spent his first days in captivity at Chatham naval hospital and from there he was sent to Dyffryn Aled Camp in Wales. Tholens described Dyffren Aled as one of the best-guarded camps in Britain, probably because it held submarine officers. He planned to escape by being taken off the Welsh coast by German submarine. Some of the prisoners in the camp who had lived in England before the war were repatriated at Christmas, 1914, and Tholens had sent a message with one of them. This was answered in a communication hidden in letters and it was arranged that a German submarine would be there to pick Tholens and another submarine captain up in August. The two men managed to get out of the camp by cutting through an iron bar on a window. They walked through the night to reach the sea by the morning. It was evident how easy it was for escaped prisoners to be at large in the country at the time as the men went to a restaurant in Llandudno for breakfast. They spent two nights at Great Ormes Head where they tried to signal the submarine that was supposed to have met them. They got no reply on the first occasion and the same thing happened the following night. Tholens found out later that the submarine was there, but was very close in shore and they were unable to see each other due to the high cliff. The men tried to make their way to London instead, but were caught at the station in Llandudno.

Despite the supposed contentment of the military prisoners in Britain a number continued to escape. There were many who thought that it was their duty to try and return to the war. Two prisoners had escaped from the camp at Oldcastle as well as three from the camp at Duffryn Aled. The latter three were soon recaptured and sent to Chester Castle, which it seems was more secure.

There was a rather different aspect to the men who escaped from the Oldbury Camp in County Meath, Ireland. Mr Charles Fox, who lived in the town, was arrested by the military authorities soon after the escapees were captured. Fox was described in the press as a well-known nationalist whose house was searched after the prisoners escaped. He was charged with aiding and abetting the escape and was taken under arrest to Dublin. There were constant rumours of connections between Irish nationalists and Germany. The presence of German prisoners in Ireland must have been a temptation for the nationalists looking for allies.

Escapes of military prisoners continued, including two officers from Donington Hall, which was still claimed to be a luxurious home for German officers. Descriptions were given of the two men in the press. They were Otto Thelen of the German Flying Corps and Hans Kellack, a naval lieutenant. Both were later recaptured in the Chatham district.

There was also an escape of five men from Dorchester camp. Edwin Bergmen and Hans Heym were both officers and Heym was the pilot of a German seaplane that had crashed in the North Sea. Airmen were well represented in the number of escapees, despite their numbers being low compared with other prisoners. The two men were captured at Hartlepool Docks trying to stow away on a ship. They were both charged with entering a restricted area. Two more of the escapees from Dorchester were caught on a train from Moreton to Waterloo. Both men, Walter Iven and Joseph Strutman, who had been a crew member on a submarine, had third-class tickets for the train. The fifth man named Dalker was still at large. The two men, caught at Hartlepool, were dealt with in court charged with entering a restricted area. It was said in court that Bergmann and Heym had been in London and Deal while free before they went to Hartlepool. They were both sentenced to six months hard labour.

It is recorded that many enemy prisoners of war had English, Welsh or Scottish accents, having lived in Britain before the war. When the British ship *Arethusa*, part of the Harwich Force, went to rescue survivors from the *Blücher*, one of the German seamen was hauled on board by a British stoker named Nobby Clark. The German said, 'Hello, Nobby. Fancy seeing you here'. The two men had been next-door neighbours in Hull before the war.

There are numerous examples of prisoners of both sides being treated very well at sea. For example, prisoners would at times be put on board fishing boats so that they could be picked up by their own side later. Admiral Tyrwhitt, the commander of the Harwich Force, said, 'the Huns treated our prisoners very well. They said that they knew we had been very kind to their prisoners'. When the German U-boats were surrendered at Harwich at the end of the war, Tyrwhitt ordered his men not to celebrate in front of the German.

The British press were always very keen to publish stories about large numbers of prisoners being taken by one or very few men. It seems that this was also common in Germany and a letter from a German soldier concerning this was also published in the *New York Times Current History Magazine*. The man in question was wounded and in hospital and was laughing at a story in a newspaper about one German soldier surrounding thirty Russians and taking them prisoner. The man claimed that he later went on to capture 210 Russians and a baggage train of thirty wagons with only two men. The incident occurred at Eydtkuhmen where he saw Russian soldiers setting fire to houses. Three Russians came out of a house and ran straight into the three German soldiers and they surrendered. He told them to tell their men that there were five machine guns in the woods and a large party of Uhlans. The Russians then all surrendered, there were 210 of them and the baggage train. The three German soldiers then came under fire from another thirty Russian soldiers in a trench. Leaving his two men to watch the prisoners he drove the baggage train back to his division. The major in charge could not believe what he was seeing and then the other two men turned up with the crowd of prisoners—it seems as if the men were happy to surrender.

It seems there was a change of heart in the treatment of prisoners in Germany in August. Mr J. W. Gerard, the American ambassador in Berlin, claimed that the German authorities were satisfied that German prisoners in England were being treated as well as the conditions could permit. However, they were still not happy with prisoners being held on ships.

In Germany, there were plans in place to train a number of commiserate officers in how to run prisoner of war camps. Running a camp was a new experience as there had never been so many prisoners taken in any former conflict. There had already been an improvement in the food given to the prisoners. The ambassador attended one of the lectures on running camps and was suitably impressed.

The case of a man who claimed not to be a German was heard before the Lord Chief Justice in August. The man was Mr Percy Carlbach whose father Henry had become a naturalised British citizen in 1869. Before he died in 1909, however, he had been re-naturalised as a

German. Percy Carlbach had been born in Germany in 1884 when his parents were on a visit to the country. He only returned to England in 1909. He claimed that he was never a German citizen, but it was decided that he was not British either.

The appeals against internment were a long drawn-out process. Many had applied as early as May, but, in late September, up to 800 more aliens were interned at Alexandra Palace and Stratford. They were taken to the camps in buses from London police stations. These were the applicants whose appeals were refused. Many of these had appealed to the Home Office when told they would be arrested, but were informed that the decisions of the committees were final.

One of the internment camps was visited in September by Mr John Van der Vour, London editor of the *Amsterdam Telegraaf* along with two American journalists. The camp was at Islington in the old St Mary Institute for the Poor, which had previously served as a workhouse. Aside from a few police officers at the door, there were no guards for the 700-plus prisoners. The internees were described as of military age and of all social classes. The men managed the camp themselves and each section had its own captain. They shared the work of the camp, but there were 160 men who paid 2s and 6d a week so that they did not have to do any work. It was these well-off men who were also the main customers for barbers who had set up their own shops in the camp. The kitchen was managed by a former London chef and four meals a day were provided. The internees were allowed weekly visitors. There was tennis, croquet, skittles and chess for the men to play, and theatrical and musical performances. Unlike military prisoners they were allowed newspapers. Some of the men were even allowed to attend to business matters and leave the camp on some days.

The Manchester Guardian reported on German claims that German women and children in England were being left to starve. They explained how when the war began the leading alien relief societies formed the Central Council of the United Alien Relief Societies. Up to the middle of August they had collected more than £33,000 from the British public, which seemed to show that not everyone was as anti-German as some of the newspapers claimed. The secretary of the Central Council Mr W. J. Cable said that by July 20,000 enemy aliens had been cared for and that they were now supporting 450 alien families every week. They were given free maternity care, free boots and clothing, and they were also supporting those women who were being repatriated. The women were given free escorted transport to Tilbury.

The early air raids in the east end of London had attracted sightseers from the better-off parts of the city. It was not to be very long before they did not have to go looking for bomb damage as the air raids also reached the west end. On 13 October one of the most serious air raids so far took place in the heart of London's theatre land. On that night seventy-one died and 128 were injured. There were a number of revellers out on the streets, despite previous raids and the darkness of the streets—due to the Defence of the Realm Act that restricted lighting. There were lights in the sky, but these came from searchlights seeking out enemy airships. When the bombs began to fall there was panic in the streets. A bus was blown up in Aldwych and large crowds in a narrow street between the Lyceum and Covent Garden were devastated when a bomb landed amongst them. In some theatres the show went on as the cast attempted to try and calm the audience and stop them from rushing out into the chaos on the streets.

There was another event in October that added to the hatred of Germany. The British nurse Edith Cavell was shot for helping British soldiers to escape from Belgium. The shooting of a woman was a terrible move in the propaganda war for the Germans. They did not seem to have the same level of understanding of propaganda as the Allies. The French had supposedly already executed two female German spies before Cavell was executed, but this was not used as a defence of the German actions. I say supposedly because the number of women executed by the French for spying is unclear. There is no doubt that they later executed Mata Hari, Maguerite Francillard, and Antoinette Tichelly, among others. There are no definite records of how many women the French did execute during the war and the reported numbers vary enormously according to various sources. Some claim that the number was at least in double figures.

Mr John Van der Veer who had visited both British and German prisoner of war camps in the past was at Dorchester Camp in December. The London editor of the *Copenhagen Telegraaf* was accompanied by a number of American journalists. He reported that there were 3,400 prisoners in large barracks that had been used for cavalry before the war. A number of wooden huts had been added to the site. The camp was near the old Roman fort site. The prisoners were allowed to speak to Mr Van der Veer in German and told him that they were satisfied with their treatment, food, and accommodation. Most agreed that the British treated them fairly, with only one man refusing to answer. One man complained that the soup was very thin. The camp commandant agreed with him and the German cooks were replaced. There were only a few officers and sergeants and about twenty guards at the camp. There were pianos in some of the rooms and there were frequent concerts by a prisoner orchestra. The instruments had been sent from home or supplied by the guards. They mainly played German music. All the men had received an overcoat when arriving at the camp. Those who worked received 6s a week, but there were no compulsory occupations. The men were taken for walks outside the camp three times a week for exercise. There had been complaints from Germany that some of the prisoners in the camp had been living in tents; representatives from the Red Cross were sent to investigate this rumour and found that all the inmates were in huts and it was the guards who were living in tents. One of the Americans commented that the English treat their prisoners very well.

There was also a visit to Alexandria Palace, by a man described as a neutral writer, just before Christmas. This was still a civilian internment camp, not a military one. He said that several well-dressed women had entered the camp in front of him carrying parcels. There were a number of men and women examining objects in large glass cases. These contained carved boxes, model ships, and numerous other items made by the internees in the workshops that were available to them. Not only were the men allowed visitors, but they could also leave the camp on occasions to visit sick relatives. There were around 3,000 prisoners in the palace who were divided into three battalions. The administration of the camp was the responsibility of captains elected by the prisoners. The great halls of the building had been turned into dormitories. There was no compulsory work and there were a number of options available to the men to pass the time, including German books and access to newspapers. As with other camps they had their own orchestra. Many carried on their own occupation including tailors, boot makers, and barbers. Professors gave lectures and some even continued with their research while interned. It was an ideal opportunity for the psychological study of the effects of confinement on the person. Since the escape from the camp the number of guards had been increased and the visitor was often challenged by guards with fitted bayonets as he toured the halls.

Personal memories of guards at internment camps or POW camps in Britain are rare, but Robert Graves did record his memories of being in a camp in his autobiography. When Graves enlisted as a lieutenant he was sent to the internment camp at Lancaster, which was situated in a disused wagon works. There were around 3,000 prisoners and he said that many were resentful of their treatment as a large number were family men who missed their wives and children. They were seen as safer inside the camps after the outbreaks of violence against aliens, but still missed their families. One of the internees was named Herr Wolff who alleged that he was taken to the camp handcuffed by fifty armed police. He also claimed that there were children held in the camp. The claims were later published in *The Times* and were ridiculed. Graves however confirmed Wolff's assertions and said that he was there when Wolff arrived with the armed police and confirmed that they were handcuffed. He also said that there were children held in the camp for a time, but did not say why or for how long. Graves also described the guards at the camp who were mainly special reservists. He alleged that they were scared of the prisoners and spent much of their time off duty drinking. There were a number of German seamen in the camp and Graves claimed that they often fought amongst themselves. There do not seem to be many other reports of prisoners fighting amongst themselves, although there are some. The continuing seclusion of those who were seen as enemy aliens continued with even men from the highest echelons of society included. Sir Felix Semon had been court physician to Edward VII; he claimed that he was being boycotted by his adopted country because he had been born a German. He declared that he was living the life of a hermit.

3

1916

The year of 1916 was to see a great advance in medical treatment for British troops with the first non-direct blood transfusion carried out by the Royal Army Medical Corps—the first non-direct blood transfusion had been carried out the previous year. Medical advancements were badly needed with the huge battles that took place in Verdun and the Somme in 1916. There was trouble at home when there was an uprising in Dublin with a number of deaths on both sides. Tanks were used by the British for the first time and Lord Kitchener died when the ship he was travelling on was sunk by a German torpedo.

The beginning of the year introduced the concept of conscription. The idea of forcing men into the Army went against the British ideals of freedom, but there was no choice because of the shortage of manpower. Many of the freedoms that the British people had been used to were restricted during the war, so conscription was not an entirely unexpected development.

The Military Service Act became law at the end of January and every British male subject between the age of eighteen and forty-one, unmarried with no dependants, was to be enlisted for service. This was to be a further cause for resentment by sections of the population against those aliens who were not interned, but who could go on with their lives, such as they were, while the British men were forced to join the services.

As the war progressed, and the U-boat blockade began to affect food supplies and rations within the camps began to decline. The amount of food given was calculated according to the number of calories it included. Vitamins had yet to be discovered. The calorie intake was regulated, but the quality of the food that contained the calories wasn't. The internees, of course, saw the decline in the amount of food as bad treatment, and food became more important in the camps than money—you couldn't buy food if there was none to be had no matter how rich you were. Another reason given for the decline in rations was that it was a reciprocal action, responding to a decline in the amount of food given to British prisoners abroad. By this time all countries involved in the war interred their hostile aliens, and the reason given for all changes in treatment was that it was merely a response to enemy actions. Another factor was press stories, especially in the newspapers owned by Lord Northcliffe who was later appointed Director for Propaganda by Lloyd George. Having been instrumental in encouraging internment, sections of the press now went on to suggest that British prisoners were being treated badly while Germans in Britain were living a life of luxury. It seems strange that if the interned were living a life of luxury then they should want to escape from it. It seemed that many did; it was heard in the Manx House of Keys that an extensive and skilful tunnel had been dug at Knockaloe Camp and was discovered by accident. A number of prisoners who had escaped and been recently recaptured and had in their possession large amounts of provisions. A public enquiry was called for respecting camp management and it was urged that the use of money by prisoners should be strictly prohibited.

Internment in other countries was different to that in Britain. There had been 400,000 people of German origin in Canada at the outbreak of war and there were also around 200,000 Austrians and Hungarians. Many of these had been working on Canada's new railway systems. As work ended the men drifted into the towns and the vast majority of the aliens were never interned. To free the towns of these enemy aliens, eighteen internment camps were set up in some of the most remote parts of the country. The actual numbers interned were low with less than 2,000 Germans in camps and slightly more Austrians. Unlike the internees in Britain, those in Canada were set to work straight away. They were used to clear forests and build roads and many of them also worked on the harvests on farms. The vast majority of foreign nationals in Canada were free throughout the war. There was no interference with enemy aliens who were law abiding, although they did have to surrender any firearms that they owned. The Canadian system would have perhaps been similar to what would have happened in Britain without such public and media pressure.

Not only were the interned aliens living a life of luxury, they were, according to some, being paid for it. A letter to *The Times* in January from H William Cooper, president of the Southend Chamber of Commerce, questioned the large amounts of money being paid to aliens who had suffered loss in the riots of the previous year. According to Mr Cooper it was well known that the German scheme of espionage included establishing spies in the commercial life of local communities. Therefore, it should not be the duty of any ratepayer to recompense anyone who showed the least suspicion of being included in this scheme. I am not sure where the proof for Mr Cooper's claims came from, but the majority of those aliens attacked were guilty of nothing more than being foreign. He seemed to believe that it was their own fault that they were attacked. Another person who had been a self-elected spokesman for those opposed to all aliens was Mr Joynson-Hicks, MP for Brentford. At the beginning of 1916 he was still complaining about the 12,000 aliens still at large in the country, many living in sensitive areas. When asking a question about these in the Commons he was told that it was common knowledge that those aliens living in restricted areas had permission from both the Home Office and the consent of the local chief constable of police.

What the population often overlooked was that many of the men who were interned had wives and children left outside of the camps; with the breadwinner interned it usually left the families outside of the camps destitute. With no money permitted to be sent from Germany, many of these families were helpless. The feeling of enmity towards aliens also led to a lack of support for these families from their neighbours. Those who sought help from the Society of Friends often had an average length of residence in England that was more than eighteen years. Some had lived here much longer, often up to forty years. The longer these people had lived here the greater the number of their English grandchildren grew. The majority of the alien families who had become destitute due to internment were from middle-class families. Their fall had therefore been greater than if they had already been living in poverty in slums. This was a problem; the families often lived in expensive houses and they realised that they had to face eviction so that cheaper accommodation could be found. This in itself was then difficult as landlords would not take in aliens.

There was an allowance that was paid to the foreign wives of interned men from their own country. This was paid through the German and Austrian embassy's, but was then arranged through the

American embassy once the German and Austrian ones closed. The allowance was minimal and had to be repaid after the war. If they could not repay it many did not apply for it. In the case of English wives of aliens the British government did pay them an allowance, which was slightly more than foreign wives received. This was paid through the Poor Law Guardians and the regulations were worded that they may give up to such an amount if deemed necessary. To get this minimal amount they had to prove they were British, married, and that their husband was interned. The process was intentionally made very difficult.

In London the weekly grant was at first set at 10*s* for a wife and 1*s* and 6*d* for a child under fourteen years. It was later raised to 12*s* and 6*d* for the wife and 3*s* for children. Outside London the rate was lower; one woman with six children received £1 and 2*s* a week. The rent, gas, bread, fuel, insurance, and shoe leather she had to pay for came to 18*s* and 6*d* leaving her with 3*s* and 6*d* for food. One woman lost her grant when her husband died while interned. She got work in Kew, which was beyond her 5-mile limit as she lived in central London. This meant that every time she went to work she had to get permission from the police station and obtain a permit, which then had to be returned to the station every evening.

There was an example of how camps differed when Mr W. Hughes of the Society of Friends visited Alexandra Place in February. He spoke to a man who had been in Knockaloe Camp who had come to London to visit his dying wife and was then sent to Alexandra Palace. He said he preferred Knockaloe as living with twenty men in a hut section was like living in a family, but at Alexandra Palace hundreds of men were kept together and could not get away from each other.

There was a move to send men with English wives who came from London back to Alexandra Place from the Isle of Man. The government did it seems have some compassion and thought that it would be better for those whose wives were still in the country to be close to their husbands so that they could visit. In later cases this was reversed and men from camps in London with wives were sent to the Isle of Man.

The children of German parents living in Britain had various experiences. A number of them joined the Middlesex Regiment in 1916 and were formed into two labour battalions; the 30 and 31 Battalions were promised that they would not have to bear arms against Germany and served in the United Kingdom. Some of these men had German connections still. Hugo Hotopf was born in Britain of German naturalised parents. He worked in a chemical works in Germany before the war and then in a similar job in London. In 1916 he applied for exemption from military service on the grounds of his important work. This was refused and he was enlisted into the Middlesex Regiment, but after the war he still kept up his close association with Germany.

Four German seamen who escaped from Knockaloe Camp on the Isle of Man in January were close to getting back to Germany. They had managed to board a fishing vessel at Peel Hill. They were then spotted by two fishermen who raised the alarm. The boat was immediately surrounded by the police and the military while another fishing boat blocked the mouth of the harbour. The men were then returned to their camp. There was also an escape by two men from Oldcastle in Ireland. Descriptions of the two men, August Boykreyer and Karl Graurnam, were given in the national press.

There was a novel attempt to get out of being interned by a man who claimed to have no nationality at all. The strange case of Emil Simon was heard at the High Court in London. Simon had been charged at Marlborough Street police station in July, 1915, for failing to register as an enemy alien. Simon claimed that he was not an enemy alien. He was born in Saxe-Coburg in 1887 and then immigrated to America. In 1891 he had received a document from the State Ministerial Office of Saxe-Coburg certifying that he had been discharged from the nationality of Saxe-Coburg. Simon also presented a certificate of nationalisation from the superior court of New York, which was dated 1894. After many years working in London, an application to the American Consulate led to the rejection of his request to be registered as an American citizen. Simon was then found guilty and fined £5. Simon was not the only person to end up in court over the uncertain rules on aliens. At Bow Street police court in July, John Dallas (a clerk to an alien's inspector at the Home Office) and Noi Atlanti, alias Altschuler (a Russian), were charged with money being corruptly paid to Dallas as a public officer. Atlanti had been charging Ottoman Jews for permits to leave the country. He did this by pretending to be someone of influence in the Home Office. Restrictions on this group leaving the country had already been lifted. Dallas as part of his duties had in his possession a list of Jews who had been refused permission to leave the country before the rules had been changed. Suggested by Dallas, Atlanti_had formed a society to obtain Ottoman Jews Spanish nationality in order to leave the country. He then charged around £100 for using his influence at the Home Office to obtain them permits to leave. Dallas at first denied involvement, though later confessed. Before passing sentence, Mr Justice Low said that it was the boast of this country that its officials were incorruptible, a fact that in no small part was the cause of their dominion over eastern races. Dallas was sentenced to three years in prison and Atlanti was sentenced to twelve months' hard labour and to be deported when his sentence was complete.

While at Knocklaoe camp, Paul Cohen-Portheim applied to move to a gentleman's camp. There were two of these at Douglas and at Lofthouse Park and although he didn't think he would be sent to one he was eventually moved to Lofthouse Park, near Wakefield—the camp was a bit of a disappointment. The view was not as nice as it had been on the Isle of Man and he had found the variety of mixed classes in his old camp more interesting than those in the gentleman's camp who were all very similar. Cohen-Portheim seems unusual in his view as the majority seemed to think that the mixing of different classes was a terrible thing. Conditions at Lofthouse Park were better though. It cost 10s a week to stay there and the inmates could draw up to £3 a week to spend. They were allowed to buy sherry and beer from a well-stocked canteen. According to the newspapers they lived in luxury and even had a golf course, which of course wasn't true. Lofthouse Park and the officer's camp at Donington Hall seemed to be the favourite targets of sections of the British press. Cohen-Portheim commented on how internees were treated. During his time at Lofthouse Park there were three or four different commandants in command and he said that they made no difference at all to conditions in the camp. Most of the rules in the camp were enforced by their own elected hut captains and aside from a roll call they had little to do with guards or the commandants. The main problem was not how well they were treated but the fact that there was nothing to do all day. This was despite having resources such as a library, tennis court, numerous concerts by the musicians, and talks by anyone who knew anything that they could lecture on. There was an attempt to turn the camp into a university where they could learn and qualify for something by the time they left, but this was not really feasible.

There were still escapes taking place from POW camps and in February, 1916, Flight-Lieutenant Otto Thelen of the German Army

Flying Corps and Naval Lieutenant Hans Keilback were charged at Holyport Prison with attempting to escape from Donington Hall by tunnelling. After the tunnel was discovered, a Boy Scout was sent down it, to discover that it stretched for 80 yards. Despite being caught after their escape attempt, the same two men were again caught trying to tunnel out of their new camp at Philberds, near Maidenhead. The two men had been caught in the bathroom with the floor up. They were then moved to a hut, but a few weeks later one of them was caught under the bed cutting the floor while the other played a mouth organ to hide the noise.

There was a change in the rules applying to aliens early in the year. Until now all aliens living in prohibited areas had to register with the police. This would now apply to aliens everywhere except in the Metropolitan police district of London. In London only aliens of neutral nationality had to register if they moved into the district after 14 February. The effect of regulations towards aliens even had an effect on those at the highest level of society. In February, a German woman appeared at Slough Police Court; Elsie Louise Kambs was a maid for the Honourable Mrs Lyttelton, wife of the headmaster of Eton School. Kambs was charged with trying to send a secret message to Germany. The woman had been working as a maid in England for more than twenty years and had applied for a certificate of exemption from repatriation. At the time of the offence she believed that this had been refused and that she would be sent back to Germany. While visiting a German woman about to return to Germany she decided to ask her to take a letter to her sister in Germany. As she thought that she was to be repatriated the letter was about finding work back in her own country. However, it was against regulations to send any messages to Germany except through the post, where they could be censored. By the time Kambs came to court, her exemption from repatriation had been granted. As a result of her offence the exemption was cancelled and arrangements made for her to leave from Tilbury at the end of the month. She was also was fined £5.

In another court case a German subject, Alfred Stockhouse, was sent to prison for six months. Stockhouse claimed to be Danish, but had been interned early in the war. He had escaped, been recaptured, and then freed. He was later working in munitions in Leeds and had then entered the Humber area without permission. He claimed he had not been in Germany since he was nine years old and rolled up his sleeve to show a tattoo of a Union Jack on his arm.

The Times published a story from Germany where there had been claims of ill treatment of German women and children in London. This related to those who had been deported back to Germany and who it seems were interviewed at the German borders by magistrates. The claims ranged in seriousness from a boy who was given a black eye at school to a German man who was trampled to death by a mob in Piccadilly. The Foreign Office replied to the charges as either trivial or imaginary. They claimed that the reports were based on twenty-six undesirable characters out of a total of 7,000 who had been returned to Germany. A Home Office investigation found no evidence to support the claims of the death in Piccadilly.

The British government had made no denials of the spontaneous outburst of popular feeling against Germans, especially in working-class areas of London after the sinking of the *Lusitania*. The striking of a German medal to commemorate the sinking of the Lusitania had only made matters worse. In these incidents no German man, women, or child was seriously injured, but 107 police and special constables were injured and 866 persons were arrested and charged with offences. It seems that the government were under fire from both sides as soon after the complaints from Germany about ill treatment of aliens there was another claim of lax control of aliens. One of His Majesties Inspectors of Constabulary, Mr Leonard Dunning, claimed that there had been considerable laxity in the administration of the Aliens Restriction Act at Plymouth. In one case this involved either gross neglect or crass stupidity on the part of police officers in the previous year. The problem that the police had across the whole country was that their workload had increased enormously with the outbreak of war, especially in relation to the Alien Registration Act. This was despite the fact that more than 9,000 police officers had left the force to join the Army or Navy since the war had begun. As a whole, the force was more than 4,000 paid officers short, which had been made up with the introduction of special constables.

A new source of prisoners was caused through an uprising in Dublin at Easter; the government had to contend with Irish rebels who had seized various locations and declared independence for Ireland. There was said to be some level of German support for this and this was to be a continuous rumour throughout the war. There were other, smaller incidents in other parts of the country at the same time. The German involvement turned into a farce as Sir Roger Casement, a former Consul General, had returned from Berlin after asking for German help. He was landed in Ireland from a German submarine on Good Friday and captured immediately. A German cruiser disguised as a merchantman was loaded with 20,000 rifles and ammunition meant for the revolt, but was sunk by its own crew after being intercepted by the Navy. The crew were then taken prisoner and Casement's capture was announced on the day the revolt began. The rebels took control of a number of buildings, including the post office. One of those involved in the attack on the post office said that the attack took place at noon. The men who attacked were armed with pikes, shot guns, and rifles. There was a small garrison of British troops, which was quickly overcome. One old lady was very angry as she had been about to buy some stamps when the post office was taken over. The Army in Ireland could not cope with the rebellion and more troops had to be sent from England under Sir John Maxwell. A gunboat was used to shell Liberty Hall and artillery was used on buildings held by the rebels. Most of them had surrendered by 29 April. Of the surviving rebels fourteen were executed, more than seventy were sent to prison—some for life—1,706 were sent to England to be imprisoned. There had been 180 civilian deaths during the rebellion, these were both rebels and innocent bystanders, and 614 wounded, with 124 British troops killed and 388 wounded.

When an alien arrived in another city they had to register with the police. In April, French-born actress Sarah Bernhardt arrived in Birmingham to perform at the Grand Theatre. When registering, a description of the person was also logged. Bernhardt's stated that she was minus her right leg—she had lost the limb to gangrene.

There was a comical example of how the rules applying to aliens were unclear to many of the population, including those who should have known better. Sir Stuart Samuel was a magistrate, as well as an MP for Chelwood Vetchery Nutley. He was summoned before Ukfield magistrates in March for failing to notify the presence of an alien in his household. When Mr Samuel had been asked by the police why he had failed to inform them of the lady's presence he said that he didn't know that he had to. He claimed in court that he thought aliens were only those from enemy countries and had only realised that this was not the case when reading in the paper that a friend had been fined for failing to do so. The alien in question was a French Governess. The case was dismissed. The regulations regarding aliens seemed to change on a regular basis and in April they were changed so that all aliens had to register with the police and report changes of address. Those in prohibited areas also had to carry an identity book. No enemy alien above the age of seventeen was allowed at large without exemption from the Secretary of State.

There was a keen awareness amongst the public in relation to the escape of German military prisoners and it was often members of the public who were responsible for the recapture of escapees. This was the case in April when four men were recaptured on the moors in sight of Liverpool. The four men had escaped from Frongoch Camp in Merionethshire. They had managed to cross the mountains into Denbighshire and were seen on the Llandegla Moors by Mr Hugh Jones of the local post office. Mr Jones had read the men's description and was suspicious when seeing four men on the moor. He sent a message to the local police and followed the men. The men hid in heather for a time before returning to the road. They refused to speak when approached and they were eventually taken by a search party. They claimed to be Welsh and were on a trip, but then admitted their identity and that they were heading for the Mersey. There never seemed to be any attempt to evade capture by using violence in the case of escapees.

There were still regular reports of mistreatment of British prisoners being held in Germany and the *New York World* in May stated that the subject of prisoners of war would have to be seriously considered at the next Hague Conference. The report went on to say that Germany must care for more than 2 million prisoners, but this did not warrant the savage treatment of them, especially towards British prisoners. There was also a statement from Lord Newton at this time who was the Assistant Under-Secretary of State for Foreign Affairs and Prisoners of War. In the report he said that there was an element in Britain that called for retaliatory measures against German prisoners, but that the British mind did not work that way. From the beginning of the war Britain had, according to Newton, tried to maintain a sane and normal basis for prison camps. It was not true that prisoners lived in the lap of luxury, but they did lived comfortably. One of the complaints made was that prisoners were not given work to do. In Germany the majority of prisoners were made to work, sometimes in hazardous situations. Prisoners in France were also made to work, often in French ports. There was some use of the interned civilians in the Isle of Man who worked in agriculture and road making. There was a worry about using military prisoners, but the idea of using them in work outside the camps was becoming more acceptable.

There were some attempts at exchanging prisoners who were no longer able to fight due to sickness or wounds. There were British and German members of the board that decided which prisoners were eligible and there were also two Swiss members, Colonel Sturzenegger and Captain Schwyzer. They had been working in Germany in April and May, inspecting French and Belgian prisoners. Permission to also deal with British prisoners was given later and they were to return to Germany to do this. The Swiss officers were favourably impressed with the treatment of German prisoners, particularly in war hospitals. At Dartford they found the prisoners well-nourished and clean and their quarters as good as could be expected for prisoners of war. They were also impressed with the chivalrous and kindly way that the camp commandants treated their charges.

The death of Lord Kitchener on the torpedoed-ship HMS *Hampshire* was to lead to rumours amongst the population that there were some alien hands involved in the death. This was so evident that it even led to a report in *The Times* where it was hinted that the ship was on the route taken by German submarines *en route* to Ireland. There were many who believed that news of Kitchener's presence on the ship could have somehow been leaked to the enemy. This no doubt had much to do with the situation in Ireland at the time. Kitchener's death was another excuse for people to take to the streets again and show their displeasure by attacking enemy aliens. Strangely this did not include the east end of London, but took place in Acton, Tooting, and Islington. It was unusual for those patriots in the east end not to have become involved in the chance of rioting.

There was a visit to Stratford Camp in June by officials of the United States Embassy. At the time it was under the command of Lieutenant Colonel F. A. Heygate Lambert. The camp held only 174 men at the time. There were 141 Germans, thirty Austrians, and three Turks. There had been no changes in sleeping accommodation or washing facilities since the last inspection. The camp was described as comfortable, especially due to the low number of prisoners. The camp seemed to have gone through a number of different uses since it opened. It was at first described as a transit camp and most prisoners seemed to move onto the Isle of Man quickly. Others spent quite long periods there and the American inspectors said that the men there were mainly waiting to be repatriated.

The provisions of the Military Service Act were expanded in May to include married men. Despite this, the numbers of men being supplied

1. German prisoners at an English camp in France. The accommodation consists of tents, and a number of the prisoners are wounded. Many of the prisoners held in France were later sent to England.

2. German prisoners taken during an Allied advance, watched by British officers. Few of the men seem to have anything with them, apart from what they are wearing.

3. The introduction of tanks was a shock to the German troops. The first reports of their use claimed that German infantry surrendered in their hundreds at the sight of a tank.

4. German prisoners helping British guards to carry a stretcher; it is hard to see if the wounded man on the stretcher is a prisoner or a British soldier.

Above left: 5. Prisoners were often a useful source of information. This German was captured in a raid, and here he is pointing out the disposition of his unit.

Above right: 6. Some of the thousands of prisoners taken at the Battle of the Sambre. There seem to be few guards in relation to the number of prisoners.

7. A typical scene from the war, with French troops moving up towards Thiepval Ridge while German prisoners pass on the left.

8. A group of German prisoners who seem to be lining up for food; their state of dress suggests that it was summer.

9. German prisoners and guards. There seem to be some kind of shelters in the background that look like they are made of corrugated iron; they could be the prisoner's quarters.

10. A large tented camp for German prisoners on the Western Front. The men seem to have little to occupy them inside the camp.

11. The camp at Elsenborn, Belgium, was a German Army camp when they held the area; however, it was later used to hold prisoners of war.

Visé à Boulogne-sur-Mer

Campagne 1914-1915

27. *Départ de Prisonniers Allemands pour l'Angleterre*

12. German prisoners at a railway station in France, awaiting transport to England. There are few guards and some Red Cross soldiers. There are also civilians on the platform, close to the prisoners.

13. A large number of German prisoners outside in a camp. The huts for the prisoner's accommodation are visible in the background. The location of this camp is unclear.

14. The camp at Camberley. The prisoners here included seamen and soldiers. The report that accompanied this photograph said that every evening the men sang the German national anthem and prayed for German success in the war.

15. German prisoners marching from Frimley Station to Frith Hill Camp, well-guarded by armed soldiers.

16. German prisoners entering the gates of a tented camp. The report that accompanied the image states that the men were of a degenerate type and contrasted badly with the clean, alert British soldier.

17. A German camp that looks to have been erected around pre-existing buildings. The barbed-wire fence does not look as strong or as high as those at most camps.

Above: 18. The funeral of a German prisoner of war held in Handforth, Cheshire. The funerals of POWs were often attended by large numbers of locals as well as fellow prisoners.

Middle: 19. A drawing from a contemporary publication, showing the 'Happy lot of the captive Hun at Dorchester Camp'.

Right: 20. A death card for a German prisoner, Josef Müller, who died while in captivity.

21. A view of Dorchester Camp. There were a large number of huts; the town of Dorchester is visible in the background, showing how close the camp was to the locals.

22. A photograph of some of the inhabitants of the Dorchester Camp; they look relaxed in their confinement.

23. Donington Hall. This officer's camp attracted much criticism in the press as there were claims that the captive officers lived in luxury.

Above left: 24. There was a widespread fear of spies in the country during the war and there was some basis of truth in the rumours. Captain von Rintelen was a spy and was arrested on a ship as it docked in London. He later admitted that the British secret service knew every action that German Naval intelligence had undertaken during the war.

Above right: 25. The boat deck of the *Lusitania*, where much of the tragedy of the ship's sinking took place; the disaster had a severe adverse effect on the German people living in Britain. The German Embassy had placed an advertisement in the press for the liner's journey, warning that it may be sunk.

26. The conditions in the internment camp at Ruhleben was often criticised by the British press. Inmates at the camp said that the conditions had only been poor for a short time after the camp opened. Sport was a main way of passing the time for the internees, as this image of a boxing match in the camp shows.

27. Newly interned men on their way to one of the new camps. Many of the men are carrying their belongings with them. The number of armed guards (with fixed bayonets) seems excessive for civilians, especially when military prisoners seem to have been guarded by much smaller numbers.

28. Southend, Essex, was to play a part in the war as the site of a number of air raids and of three ships used as internment camps. Here, armed guards line the streets of the town as a large number of internees march from the station to the pier.

29. A group of internees who had been arrested in Scarborough and were being taken to York. Some of the group seem quite happy at the prospect.

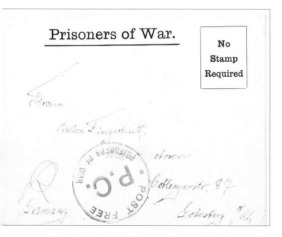

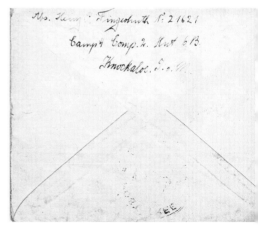

Above left: 30. The envelope of a letter from an internee to Germany. It was marked with a post-free prisoner of war stamp in red, as well as having 'Prisoners of War' written across the top of the envelope.

Above right: 31. The reverse of the envelope, with the prisoner's number, compound and hut number at Knockaloe camp on the Isle of Man.

32. The Cunningham Holiday Camp on the Isle of Man operated from the late nineteenth century. During the First World War it was taken over and converted into one of the island's internment camps.

33. Dublin after the Easter Rising of 1916, which led to a large number of Irish internees joining the enemy ones already in camps.

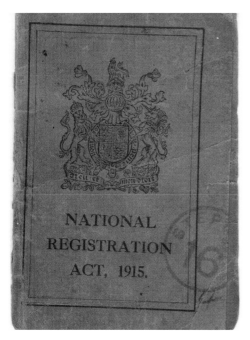
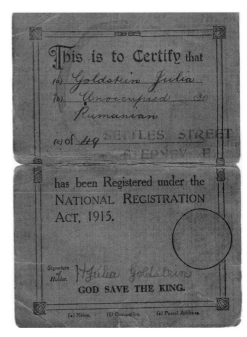

Above left: 34. A National Registration Act card from 1915. The act was an attempt to find out how many people were in the country, and it was also a useful way to find out which men had not enlisted in the forces.

Above right: 35. The inside of the card listed the person's name, address, and nationality, which in this case was 'Rumanian'. The problem with the card was that it did not include a photograph, so it could be passed on to anyone.

37. The grounds of Alexandra Palace, which had been a popular entertainment location in London until it was closed soon after the war began.

37. Alexandra Palace, which was used to house Belgian refugees before becoming one of the best-remembered internment camps—a use that was not popular with local people.

38. A workshop in Alexandra Place for the internees. It was found that those who used the workshops were much less likely to suffer from mental health problems such as barbed wire disease.

39. Some of the items that were made in the workshops at Alexandra Palace. Similar items were made in many other camps in the country.

40. The kitchens at Alexandra Palace, where the internees did their own cooking. Often the cooks were men who had worked as chefs at some of the best hotels in London.

to the Army was still not enough. This led to the government decision to remove the exemptions of many workers who could easily be replaced, in many cases by women, and to enlist them into the Army. The introduction of large numbers of women into the workforce led to a higher level of independence for them and provided them their own income. The wearing of trousers by women was a new thing as was smoking in public.

There were some conflicting views given of friendly aliens in June. There were moves towards allowing these men to join the Army. The men in question were Russian Jews who could apply through the Jewish War Services Committee, which would process their applications. In some cases these men had younger brothers in the Army who had been born here while they arrived with their parents from other countries. A few days following the permission for Russian Jews to join the British Forces was issued, a Russian Jew found himself in Marlborough Road police court. Lewis Litcock was the licensee of the Diamond Reign public house in Fourbert's Place, Regent Street, and he was charged with selling liquor during prohibited hours. The house was frequented mostly by foreigners and had a bad name because it was previously run by a German. There did not seem to be any attempt to differentiate between the fact that the previous landlord was an enemy alien and the present a friendly one in the newspaper reports. There was another example of how the labelling of aliens was difficult when Frederick Luft appeared at Wimbledon Police Court in June charged with being an absentee from military service. Luft claimed that he was the son of an unnaturalised German and that he was therefore exempt from military service. The magistrate said that if he was English he was liable for service and if German he should be interned. As a test case the decision was pending. There was a solution to the problem of whether a person was an enemy alien put forward by Chester Town Council in June. They called on the government to intern all enemy alien subjects in the country on account of their being a menace and a danger and when Mr Brown said that 'they were interfering with matters that did not concern them,' and Mr Dodd said 'could we add that all those who have sympathies with aliens be interned with them'.

There is no doubt that there were some spies operating in the country during the war and some of these were not only held at the Tower of London, but were executed there. A member of the Honourable Artillery Company, J. B. Sterndale Benet, spent part of his early military career guarding those at the Tower who were suspected of spying. He guarded a Dutchman who had been sentenced to death; the man was allowed a last visit by his wife. While leading the weeping woman away from her husband for what she thought would be the last time the sergeant major told her that what she needed was a nice cup of tea. The guards were sad about the condemned man who they had become fond of and were glad when he was reprieved at the last minute.

There was a question asked in Parliament about prisoners of war being allowed parole from the Cornwallis Road internment camp, Islington. Some prisoners were allowed out for a few hours for special reasons such as visiting sick relatives, attending a funeral, or to receive hospital treatment. There were also some business reasons, such as to sell their effects to aid the support of their families.

A large scale attack was planned in France and some thought it would end the war. The great push on the Somme was intended to have been a great success with an extended barrage that destroyed the wire, allowing the advancing Allied troops to take German trenches battered into submission. This was not what happened. The number of casualties inflicted in the attack became clear. Many of the enemy had been safe in deep bunkers and came out to fire on advancing British troops who were caught up on wire that had not been destroyed. This was not seen as the case in *The Illustrated War News*. They published an article in July showing the German prisoners taken during the opening of the battle. According to the report, the prisoners were those who surrendered in their dug outs, unnerved and dazed by the fearful ordeal of the bombardment. The claim was that even those who did put up a fight gave up as the Allies advanced. There were many prisoners taken in some areas where the advance did make some progress. Many were taken by the new secret weapon—the tank. The majority of the German prisoners taken were held in France in a large camp at Meaulte, near Albert. This camp was swamped with the large number of prisoners taken during the advance and many of them were quickly moved and taken back across the Channel to England within a few days of capture. There was no doubt of the many prisoners taken and the report went on to show large crowds of Germans being marched through Southampton a few days after the battle began. They landed at the port on 4 July. The numbers taken were given as 6,000 and of those landed at the port thirty were officers and 1,500 other ranks. Many had handkerchiefs covering their heads instead of caps. The prisoners were described as dejected or indifferent. *The Illustrated*

War News made a great deal of how chivalrous the British troops were towards their captors. In one case the British troops presented arms to the Prussian Guard who surrendered at Orvillers in recognition of their gallantry. The report also published a photograph of British soldiers lighting a cigarette for a wounded German prisoner. A number of the prisoners were put to work as stretcher bearers, carrying their own and British wounded back from the front. This was after they had been questioned and searched. Many of the prisoners had been very thirsty as their water supply had been disrupted by the Allied barrage.

The *War Illustrated* published photographs and artist impressions of a number of incidents involving the prisoners taken on the Somme. They claimed that the prisoners were unanimous in their experience of the terrible work of the British artillery fire. Many of the men who escaped death were said to be too dazed to be able to defend themselves.

They reported on one incident at Montauban, in which Germans came out of their dug out and went down on their knees, begging for mercy. The magazine published an artist's impression of 600 German prisoners being guarded by three jocks, an event supposedly witnessed by an unnamed officer. Other reports showed terrified Germans in dug outs up to 18 feet underground who surrendered before they were attacked in their holes by grenades. In another incident forty Germans, including an officer, were said to have surrendered to four Yorkshire men. The subject of numerous newspaper articles was the surrender of numerous Germans after the prolonged artillery barrage before the large attack on the Somme. What few seemed willing to mention was that in numerous places the Germans came out of their dug outs happy to carry on fighting, especially where the bombardment had done little to cut the wire in front of their trenches.

The claims of kindly treatment of prisoners were not shown in July towards Alexandre Livventaal. Mr Livventaal was of Finnish origin and was born in Switzerland. He became a naturalised British subject in 1914 and his sponsors included Mr Arthur Balfour, first Lord of the Admiralty and Admiral Sir Charles Ottley. Livventaal was an aeronautical engineer and had been sent to Switzerland as a King's Courier during the war. Livventaal travelled from Brighton to London every day, but on one occasion he was arrested by a non-commissioned officer on suspicion of being a German spy at the train station. He was marched to another platform where he was taken under arrest to Lewes and marched to the military prison. While at the gate he had to be protected from a hostile crowd by his armed escort using their bayonets. When brought before the commandant of the prison his papers were not examined as it was seen to be obvious that he was a spy from the look of his face. He was locked in a cell until the police arrived who released him straight away.

There was finally a move towards allowing friendly aliens who had been interned to work on farms in July. These included Poles, Czechs, Croats, and Armenians who were enemies only in a technical sense. Farmers who were short of labour could employ them, but had to find them board and lodgings and pay the going rate of wages. The employers had no liability as to their imprisonment apart from ensuring that they reported to the police at intervals.

Not all the registered aliens volunteered to be interned and a number of these were found in London. Edward Jansen had registered as German at the outbreak of war and should have been interned in July 1915, but he disappeared. He was then captured and said his name was Edward Wilson and claimed he was a Dane. Jansen also claimed to be Gottlieb Hefferson, a Swiss subject, and he had Swiss papers. He had acquired the papers from the real Hefferson, a Swiss valet at the Savoy Hotel. Hefferson claimed that he met Jansen in the street crying and feeling sorry for him, sold him his papers so he could go to America. It was later proved that Jensen had once lived in a restaurant that Hefferstein worked in and had known him all along. It was claimed that there was a regular traffic in these Swiss documents to enemy aliens.

A number of the internment camps in Britain were inspected by reporters from *The Times* in July. Knockaloe Camp in the Isle of Man consisted of a barbed wire enclosure about 4 miles in circumference. It was divided into four sub camps with a total of twenty-three compounds. Each compound could hold a thousand prisoners; at the time of inspection it held 22,000. The commandant was Lieutenant Colonel F. W. Panzera, CMG. For many years he had been resident commissioner of Bechuanaland. Each compound was self-contained with its own work rooms, kitchen, canteen, and bathrooms. Flour was given to each compound to make their own bread and if not used, it could be sold back to the government; the money was used in improving the diet of the prisoners. There were vegetable gardens in the camp, though there was little work for the prisoners to do outside the camp due to lack of need for extra-agricultural labour on the Isle. Some Hungarians did some turf cutting and stone breaking outside the camps. Some of the prisoner's wives had settled on the island so that they could visit their husbands on a regular basis.

The camp at Douglas was different from Knockaloe in that some of its inhabitants were from a privileged class—around 500 men from its total of 2,750. They paid 10s to £1 a week for better food and more comfortable accommodation. This could be a one fifth share of a cubicle or half a bell tent with a wooden floor. The camp had been the Cunningham summer camp for tourists before the war. It included a billiard room, concert hall, and a swimming pool. Jews in the camp had a kosher kitchen and the Roman Catholics had their own chapel. The camp commandants came from various backgrounds; the commandant of St Mary's Institute, which was once a workhouse in Islington, was Major Sir Frederick Halliday, formerly commissioner of police in Calcutta. The guards consisted of one sergeant and four police constables for more than 700 prisoners.

There was a difference between internment and prison camps, which was shown by a visit to Donington Hall. This was also an opportunity to prove that the prisoners in the stately home were not living in luxury as was often claimed. It was a camp for officers and the reporter who visited it said that if there was ever any basis for the view that the officers lived in luxury it was not evident now. The senior officers lived in the house, which was described as large and hideous. There were eight to fourteen beds in each room. The reporter described it as similar to his public school. There were five wooden huts in the grounds for junior officers. There were a total of 247 officers and sixty soldier servants in the camp, with numerous sentries and plenty of barbed wire. The commandant was Lieutenant Colonel F. S. Pigot. There were five roll calls a day and the prisoners were also checked during the night. The prisoners were paid, captains and above received 4s and 6d, and the lower ranks received 4s. They paid for everything including food, but used metal tokens instead of cash to buy from the canteen. Although it was reported that the prisoners could buy spirits, only wine was on sale and they were limited to spending a shilling a day on wine.

The camp at Leigh was for NCO's and enlisted men. It was based in a building built at the outbreak of war as a weaving shed. It was divided into seven dormitories and held more than 1,500 men. The NCO's had a screened off sections at the end of the dormitory. The commandant Colonel H. J. Blagrove, CB, ensured the strictest discipline. The prisoners were not paid, but often received money from Germany and could spend this in the canteen; however, unlike officers they could not buy alcoholic drinks. There was an emergency committee to look after the interests of the destitute.

In Scotland there were two transit camps for internees at Maryhill Barracks, Glasgow, and at Redford Barracks, Edinburgh. The internees could be held at these camps for up to four weeks, sleeping on sacks of straw. The guards were not much better off than the prisoners with similar accommodation. The main camp in Scotland was Stubs, which held both civilian and military prisoners, but in separate compounds. Although many from the Scottish transit camps did end up in Stubs, others were sent to camps all around England, which made visits from their family's very difficult.

Not all the prisoners taken were sent to Britain. Apart from those taken on the western Front who remained in France there were large numbers of prisoners in other parts of the world. The Turks captured in the Dardanelles were sent to camps close to the fighting. The press were always eager to show how well the prisoners were treated and *The Illustrated War News* said of the Turks in one camp that their considerate treatment is something unknown to them in their previous existence. German prisoners taken by the French were quickly put to work. A large number were sent to work in quarries at Royanmoix and were guarded by Algerian soldiers. Others were set to work at harbours and on coastal reclamation. These workers were housed in cargo ships moored at various ports.

With the troubles in Ireland at their height, it seems a strange decision to have set up camps for German military prisoners in the country. This was shown in August when, as part of an inquiry into the shooting of three men in Ireland during the insurrection, it was revealed that a rumour had been started that 600 German prisoners from Oldcastle had been released and armed and were on their way to Dublin. There were also rumours of a German landing taking place in Galway and a camp full of German soldiers would have been reliable reinforcements.

Three German prisoners had escaped from Handford Camp in Cheshire, Karl Reitz, Joseph Hanecke, and Ernest Agyl, and were recaptured while asleep. They told the policeman who found them that they were on their way to Scarborough. They offered the officer money to show them the way to the railway station. This is the only incident of prisoners offering a bribe that I have heard of. They were handed over to the military to be dealt with.

The number of prisoners taken by the Allies from July to mid-September was given as more than half a million. This was an enormous number, but the British share was the lowest total of all the Allies. The Russians had taken over 400,000, the French and Italians 33,000 each, and Britain 21,000 according to *The Illustrated War News*. Sir Douglas Haig gave the figure as nearer 26,000.

There had been a number of claims of large numbers of German prisoners being taken by small numbers of British soldiers during the Battle of the Somme in July. None of them can compare with an incident that did take place in September. Private Thomas Alfred Jones was a member of the Cheshire Regiment. Jones saw a sniper operating across no man's land and went out on his own and killed him. While doing this he was fired on by two more Germans who he also dealt with. Reaching a German trench, he single handily disarmed and took 102 men prisoner—this included officers. He then marched them back across no man's land to the British lines under shellfire. One can only guess that the men were eager to become prisoners. Private Jones was awarded the Victoria Cross.

In September, there was a protest from the Red Cross about reprisals on war prisoners. It was sent to all belligerent and neutral countries, but did not name any one country as being guilty of reprisals. The protest stated that if prisoners of war existed before they had never done so in such large numbers. It also mentioned that although camp conditions were generally improving, they had noticed a tendency for reprisals if countries believed their own prisoners were being poorly treated by the hands of their enemies. This lead to immediate recourse to the law of retaliation and acts in excess of the grievances, hoping that the severity of its reprisals will compel its adversaries to yield. This then lead to a barbarous competition, which is borne by the innocent and the helpless. The British government replied through Viscount Grey who said that throughout the conflict the British government had discounted the policy of reprisals on account of its unjust operation. His reply had to include a chance to blame it on the enemy and said that the patience of the British people was strained by a series of outrages on British prisoners and others committed by the orders of the German government. He went on to mention the sinking of the *Lusitania* and the execution of Nurse Cavell.

According to reports from the front in October, it seems that many of the enemy being taken prisoner were only too happy to give up. This was supposedly an expression of their faith in the humanitarian approach of the Allies. It would also seem to dispel the rumours of enemy prisoners being killed by the British. There has to be some doubt as to how those fighting on the western front would know how those taken prisoner had been treated. This question was answered in other theatres of war.

The Illustrated War News published a report from a Mr G. Ward Price writing from Salonika regarding the treatment of prisoners. According to Mr Ward Price, the Bulgarians taken prisoner by the Serbian army were worried about how they would be treated after they had themselves treated Serb prisoners so badly. To combat this the Serbs had 2,000 photo postcards printed showing prisoners being fed and dropped them over Bulgarian lines.

I was surprised to find that any number of visits could be made to prisoners held in Switzerland, although there was a limit placed on the number of visitors that could go to see the British men interned there. This was due to the limited availability of accommodation for visitors. There was only room for fifty at Chateau d'Oex, ten at Leysin, and none at all at Murren. Children were not allowed to visit. Only two visitors were allowed per prisoners and the prisoner had to name the two people he would like to come to see him. The British Military attaché in Switzerland would then send the names to the Prisoner of War Committee. Arrangements would then be made by the joint committee of the Red Cross and the order of St John of Jerusalem to arrange for the visit, whether the named people could pay their own expenses or not. A second group of visitors left London for Switzerland in October. The party consisted of soldiers wives. Many of them had not seen their husbands for more than two years. The women were named in the press and one said that she didn't think that they would want to come back.

November saw another large number of prisoners taken after the Battle of Beaumont Hamel. The prisoners were often held temporarily in what were no more than barbed wire cages until they could be moved to more permanent camps. One German officer who complained about this was told by a British staff officer, 'if only you had told us you were coming'.

Towards the end of 1916 the number of German military prisoners held by the British had passed 45,000. *The Times* published a story from an officer serving on the Somme who had been speaking to German prisoners still in a camp in France. He said that some of the enlisted men were glad to have been captured. One man told him that he was surprised to be captured by British troops; he still thought that they were fighting the French.

Although there had been fewer claims from Germany about the mistreatment of German prisoners in Britain towards the end of the year, they were now complaining about other enemies. In November, the German government claimed that due to the sufferings of German prisoners in Russia, Russian officer prisoners were being transferred to a camp where they would be subject to severe treatment. There did not seem to be a decline in reprisals by the Germans despite the Red Cross complaints. The use of German prisoners as workers on the land was at last near to completion by November. It was reported in Parliament that small groups of men could be used, their employer being responsible for their custody, housing, and feeding. All applications for workers were to be considered by a special committee at the War Office. This led to a great increase in the number of camps in the country as small numbers of prisoners who were living on farms meant that the farm was then listed as a POW camp.

There must have been some level of disquiet by the public at the thought of German prisoners being let out of their camps if they took seriously an article published in the *War Illustrated*. The article was entitled a study in what it called Hun physiognomy. The study of physiognomy was an idea once popular in ancient Greek culture, which believed that it was possible to see a man's character in his outward appearance. The article claimed that Germany enjoyed a reputation for the physical quality of her young manhood. The article included fourteen photographs of individual German prisoners. The fourteen were taken at random and according to the writer the faces showed traces of truculence, cunning, meanness, and animal hostility. Several were said to be marked with the features associated with criminality and some were of the idiot type.

There were further attempts to encourage Irish soldiers to turn against Britain by the Germans in November. Two Irish priests were sent into an Irish prisoner of war camp to try and convince the soldiers to release themselves from their oath of allegiance to Britain so that they could join the Irish revolutionary movement. When the priests declined to do this they were subjected to bad treatment. There was more news concerning the Irish in *The Manchester Guardian* in December. They reported on the Frongoch internment camp in Wales. The camp was based in an old distillery that had made Welsh whisky until the war began. It had been used for the early part of the war to hold Germans. At that time, there had been nearly 2,000 internees in the camp, but little had been heard of it. This changed once the camp became used for holding interned Irishmen. There had been numerous complaints to both the commandant and to the outside world; the basis for the complaints were explained by one of the inmates on his release. He said that if he had been a German soldier captured in battle then he would not have considered himself badly used. But he had been interned without trial and was then released with no explanation as to why he had been held or why he was released.

Work was going on inside some camps, although this was in many cases a form of handicraft based on the previous occupation of the internees. The designer Charles Rennie Mackintosh had furniture made at Knockaloe Camp under the direction of Charles Matt who had been a foreman in a London furniture factory before being interned. Furniture was also produced for the Friends Relief Committee for homeless people in France. The committee built homes for those who had lost theirs through the conflict and furniture from internment camps was made for these new homes. They may have been the first flat-pack furniture items as they were made to be assembled later in France.

There were three basket makers in Knockaloe who trained others to set up basket production. The willow for this was also grown on the island. The problem with all this industry was that items made in the camps could not be sold in shops or through companies, but only through personal contacts or charities to help the prisoners. This was no doubt to stop them being in competition with British companies.

There was a new order from the Secretary of State at the beginning of December that all male aliens of eighteen years and above who had not already registered must do so. They would be required to supply the registration stations with three photographs of themselves. Those with identity cards only needed to supply one photo.

At the end of the year there was a report put forward by Sir Louis Dane and Mr A. J. Sykes, MP, on a review of the permits held by aliens in restricted areas. These numbered 4,294 and the onus for proving they were not an enemy alien rested on them. The review led to the cases of sixty-six of those with permits being revoked. One unusual case of aliens in restricted areas was at Buckfast Abbey, Devon. It had been reinstated as an abbey in 1902 with mainly French monks in residence. However, in 1916, it was found that some of the monks were of German origins. They were not interned, but had to remain within the abbey grounds, which was then treated as an internment camp.

In December, major political shifts occurred with Lloyd George becoming Prime Minister, replacing Asquith. George had become Secretary of State for War following Kitchener's death, and had been seen as an opponent of war until 1909, when he attacked German aggression.

There was also a shock for many of the internees in Alexandra Palace as Christmas approached. A list was posted of men to be sent to the Isle of Man. Rudolf Rocker pleaded with the commandant for the men to be left where they were until after Christmas and although it was a War Office directive he managed to arrange it. The men whose names had been on the list had a difficult visit at Christmas knowing that it was the last time they would see their families.

4

1917

America finally joined the war in 1917. The French executed the spy Mata Hari, which was not such a public relations disaster for them as the shooting of Cavell had been for the Germans. Tsar Nicolas was overthrown in Russia and the French army mutinied, as did the Russian army later in the year. The bombing of London was by this time being carried out by the more lethal aircraft. *The Times* published a short item on Hindenburg in January, which had come through their special correspondent in Amsterdam from which much of the information on what was going on in Germany seemed to come from. According to the report, Hindenburg had inspected a large hospital on the Western Front. In the hospital were a number of wounded English officers. The head doctor tried to show the hospital in its best light and explained that a sister in the hospital had lived in England for so long that the prisoners believed that she was English. Hindenburg then demanded that the sister be moved and employed in treating German wounded. He ordered that a nurse who spoke no English should replace her because he did not want the English wounded treated better than his own soldiers.

There were other complaints from Germany in relation to prisoners. They demanded that all prisoners held near the front should be moved at least 20 miles behind the line of fire. This was mainly aimed at those held by the French. Since this was not done quickly enough for the Germans they moved a number of French prisoners close to the front line on their side.

Despite prisoners of war being used tit for tat—in the case of those close to the front—there were agreements between Germany and

Britain for badly wounded men to be exchanged. There were plans that this should be done using a British hospital ship, taking the Germans to Holland and then picking up the British prisoners from there and coming home. This had been arranged through the American embassy before diplomatic relations between America and Germany had broken down. It was then decided that this method was too dangerous due to danger from German U-boats. The plan was changed to using Dutch paddle steamers, which had been promised safe passage, but the changes led to delays that meant the exchanges took much longer to take place.

There was a big difference in the treatment of prisoners held by the French and those held by the British. Although both treated the prisoners with strict military discipline, with regular roll calls, the French prisoners were given work from early in the war. Much of this could be seen as war related work such as unloading ships in French ports. However, many of the British prisoners had no work forced upon them.

One of the ways that prisoners were taken was during trench raids. This was often used as a way of finding out who the units in the front line were facing in the enemy trenches. Charles Harrison was an Australian infantryman who took part in a raid. He described how he found himself on his own during the attack and bayoneted a German soldier. Unable to pull the blade back out of the man he fired his rifle to release it. Harrison then found two more German soldiers who he described being as only about seventeen years of age. He began to take them back, but on passing the body of the man he had killed one of the prisoners became very upset and threw himself on the body who it turned out was his brother. Harrison was the only member of the raid to take prisoners and was ordered to take them to the battalion headquarters. He asked the colonel to treat them well and they were given food and rum.

There were still questions being asked in Parliament in February concerning internment. The man asking the questions was once again Mr Joynson-Hicks. He claimed that German life continued in London with restaurants and clubs run by enemy aliens as well as a German dentist still in practice. There was also a dressmaker who boasted that he was not interned due to his highly placed customers. There had been a number of rumours of aliens not being interned due to their position in society. Joynson-Hicks claimed that there were 4,294 enemy aliens still at large in the city of which 287 were of military age. Sir George

Cave said that he had closed two alien restaurants and interned those running them. He had also interned sixteen members of various clubs and that a regulation dealing with restaurants kept by aliens was in preparation.

There was further discussion on the exchange of both military and civilian prisoners in Parliament in late February. Lord Newton gave the figures for British prisoners being held by the enemy. He believed that there were 200 British civilians interned in Austria, along with two or three officers. There were no civilian prisoners in Bulgaria, but 400–500 military prisoners. Turkey held 700 civilians, 2,000 British military prisoners, and 8,800 Indian military prisoners. Germany held 4,550 civilians and 35,000 military prisoners. These were rough numbers due to the unknown whereabouts of many missing men. There was an agreement with Austria that civilians over fifty-one years of age would be exchanged, though few had. This was due to the fact that Austria wanted 12,000 Austrian and Hungarian civilians held in Britain in exchange for 200 British civilians. However, those held in Austria were reported as being very well-treated. Agreements with Turkey and Germany relating to civilians had also not led to many of them being exchanged, but this had now stopped. Lord Newton then went on to explain that conditions in Ruhleben were not as terrible as had been reported while British internment camps were not paradise for their inmates. The visit of the Bishop of Bury who lived in Ruhleben camp and had said that conditions were not bad had led to criticism of his being pro-German. Although, there was no reason to doubt the bishop's word as to conditions at the German camp.

According to *The New York Times* there was a severe food shortage in all of Europe in the early part of the year and that this was much worse in Germany. This would then explain why those interned in the country were being kept short of food. One of the persons responsible for the article had spent time in Germany and said that there was still a large amount of waste in German restaurants. He claimed that there was less of a food shortage than it seemed and that the better-off classes in the country had plenty of food and it was only the poorer people who were short of food as they could not pay high prices. In France food was also short and there were plans to issue bread cards to the population to avoid waste. Much of the countries wheat-growing land had been lost due to the Germans holding so much of the country. In Britain the report said that there was a severe shortage of potatoes. There had so far been voluntary limitation of food, but no rationing as yet.

A discussion by the war cabinet in February showcased Germany's use of reprisals against British prisoners fooling the treatment of a German prisoner; Patzel, a German *Feldwebel*, had been convicted by a court martial in the Cameroons for having hollow-nosed and cut bullets. This was a common claim against German troops that they used these types of bullets because they caused such serious wounds. Patzel was sentenced to death, but this was commuted to twenty years in prison and he was being held at Maidstone. Germany had claimed that the commanding officer of the troops in the Cameroons said that these types of bullets were only used for killing game. They also sent a statement from a soldier who had been with Patzel stating that this was the case and called for the sentence to be rescinded—this was refused. In retaliation, Germany imprisoned two British officers, Captain Bate of the Duke of Wellington Regiment and Lieutenant Lamb of the Royal Naval Reserve; they were dressed like German military prisoners, confined in cells making sacks, and were threatened with charges for having dum-dum bullets in their luggage. There were calls for reprisals against two German officers and a claim that the two men were on their way home from West Africa. If the type of bullets were found in their luggage it was possible that they had been used for sporting purposes. This was the same reason for having them that the Germans had claimed in Patzel's case. There were even suggestions put to the cabinet that if the two British officers were sentenced to death then two German officers should suffer the same fate.

From the 17 February, the internees held in Britain were no longer allowed to receive food parcels from friends or family in England. They were still allowed to receive them from abroad if their friends and families could find any food to send. There was also no longer food available in the canteens in the internment camps and the rations they were given were cut by the war office. According to Rudolf Rocker the English press at the time were saying that the minimum calories needed per day was between 3,000 and 3,300. He claimed that they were only receiving 1,489 and that at least 12 per cent of the food they received was inedible. The camp commandant and doctor at Alexandra Palace made representations to the War Office over the condition of some of the food, but with no effect. Rocker claims that 75 per cent of the internees were ill because of the poor food they were given and had to be treated for stomach and bowel problems. The main problems were ruptures due to constipation. The food situation led to severe depression within the camps when illness was added to their other problems.

Some of the sons of German parents who had been born in Britain had been formed into two labour battalions of the Middlesex Regiment and had only been used at home. In 1917 two new labour companies were formed from the British born sons of German parents. These were used in France, but not close to the front. They became known as the Kaiser's Own and were not trusted by those in command to be entirely loyal.

There was some debate over the numbers involved in the exchange of civilians with Germany. Germany wanted to exchange a large number of those held in Britain for a much lower number of British prisoners held in Germany. It was thought that exchanging 5,000 British subjects for the 26,000 German civilians here and another 10,000 in the colonies was not fair. However, there would have been an advantage in ridding the country of so many prisoners in that it would save food and release the men needed to guard them who could be moved to other duties. There was some exchange of prisoners and as a result a larger number of British prisoners found themselves in Switzerland. These were invalids who could no longer play their part in the war and were allowed by their German captors to leave for the neutral country where they would stay until the end of the conflict. The men were welcomed by the Swiss with music and plenty of refreshments. Many were well enough to go on parade, but others were carried on stretchers. Although interned, they were held at Chateau d'Oex near Lake Geneva. They had a great deal of freedom and were able to enjoy winter sports such as ice hockey. There were also French prisoners with them

In March there were still complaints by the Germans about prisoners being held too close to the front by both the French and the British, although the statement agreed that the British treated their prisoners better than the French did. It was claimed that the Russians had held German airmen chained in dungeons. The Germans then retaliated with threats of posting both French and British prisoners close to the front. The French claimed that it was in fact the Germans who had done this first. In Parliament Mr J. F. Hope said that although reluctant to adopt retaliatory measures the government would decide on the action to be taken if the Germans carried out their threat.

Five prisoners who had escaped from Knockaloe Camp in March were soon recaptured in a small cove on the western side of the island. They were suffering severely from lack of food and the cold. The men were mainly seamen and one clerk. There was very little success achieved by any of the prisoners who did escape.

The use of prisoners as workers outside the camps was beginning to increase by March and not all of these worked close to their camp. In Lancashire about 200 men from the camp at Leigh were working near Manchester, which was about 20 miles from Leigh. The prisoners had to be taken by train each morning, accompanied by armed guards with an officer. They left the camp at 7.30 a.m. and returned at 5.30 p.m. every day, except for on Saturday and Sunday. There were other German prisoners working on what was described in *The Manchester Guardian* as the largest fruit farm in England. Instead of travelling to the farm every day, seventy-five prisoners accompanied by guards were living on the farm at the Toddington Orchards, Gloucestershire. The prisoner's camp was in the centre of the estate and it had sleeping huts, a large kitchen, and a wash house with hot and cold water.

Reports of both ill treatment and the killing of prisoners by the Turks was born from the report of Lieutenant Payne of the 13 Hussars, fighting in Mesopotamia in March. After a cavalry attack at Lajj they were driven back by a large number of Turkish soldiers. A number of the men were left on the field wounded and the dead were stripped by the Turks while the wounded were killed, according to Payne.

The Ministry of National Service began to operate in March, introducing a system of national industrial workers. This was an army of volunteers who would replace the men from industry who had gone into the forces. The hope had been for half-a-million volunteers, but the number who came forward was less than 200,000 proving the scheme unsuccessful.

In April there was much press attention given to how many German prisoners were being taken—it was claimed that nearly 20,000 were taken in April alone. Many of those captured after the battle of Arras were reported to have been half starved. They were happy to carry stretchers with either Allied or their own wounded on them. There were reports that German artillery prisoners may be attacked by their own infantry prisoners for failing them in battle.

After a visit by the Kaiser to the Western Front in 1917, there was a rumour that stated the Germans were told to hate the British, and that any British prisoners were to be treated with the utmost severity. The Kaiser's orders perhaps included members of the Empire, as 1,000 Australians, captured on the Hindenburg Line in April 1917, were given hardly any food and even the wounded were forced to march all the way to Germany. Later 110 Australians were forced to spend six days in a room 50 foot × 20 foot. They were given one slice of bread a day each and were not even supplied with blankets, despite snow falling outside. This bad treatment of Allied prisoners was used to inspire a greater fighting spirit in the men. Major General Monash, Commander of the Third Australian Division, distributed leaflets to his men describing how fellow Australians taken prisoner after the Battle of Bullecourt were starved in a dungeon. Whether this had an effect on fighting spirit is hard to judge. Or whether it had a result in how the German prisoners taken by the Australians were treated.

There are several reports of British prisoners being treated worse than other nationalities by the German prison camp guards, but day-to-day treatment seemed to be dependent on the camp commandant. Although there were inspections by the Americans before they entered the war, it seems that visits to the camps had to be planned in advance so conditions could be improved before the inspectors arrived. Often the inspectors were not allowed to speak to the prisoners, but if they did and the prisoners complained they could be punished afterwards. For example, when an inspector visited Meresburg and asked if there were any complaints three men commented on the conditions in the camp. The next day one of these was sent to the cells and given only bread and water. A number of the men inspecting camps in Germany had been American. This came to an end when America entered the war in April. The arrival of the Americans as allies was an event that was welcomed in Britain and the Lord Mayor of London flew the stars and stripes outside the Mansion House. There was a sudden demand for the American flag amongst the public and flag sellers began to appear of the streets of Britain to meet this new demand.

Although there seem to have been less cases of physical mistreatment of prisoners in British hands, there were often some quite harsh actions against them for seemingly minor breaches of the rules. One prisoner in Alexandra Palace received a parcel from family in Germany and in a pot of honey was a hidden note. The note had nothing sinister in it, but contained an intimate word that the sender was not keen on being seen by a censor. The man who received the parcel knew nothing about the note; in fact it was the first parcel he had ever received. The parcel was confiscated and he was told that he would be punished. Then the commandant asked the camp captain who was with the man if he agreed with the punishment. The captain said that he would not have taken his parcel, but would have told the man to write and explain the restriction on secret notes to his family. The commandant then agreed and allowed him to have the parcel.

There were some compassionate treatments of the prisoners by the officers in charge of them. Three men in Alexandra Palace sent a letter to the commandant asking to be shot as they could no longer stand being held in prison. The letter was dealt with by Major Mott. He told the men that the war would not last forever and gave each of the men half a crown and a packet of cigarettes. It turned out that one of the men had been on the way to Germany for an operation when interned and was in constant pain, which was one reason for his depression. One of the others had malaria and had been refused extra blankets. When the commandant heard this he gave the malaria sufferer two more blankets and sent the man waiting for an operation to the German Hospital in London where he had his treatment.

As there had been in 1916, there were a number of industrial disputes and strikes at the beginning of the year. The Prime Minister set up commissions to investigate the problems. The men's complaints were usually related to high food prices, working too many hours, and a lack of housing.

There were details in the press of how important it was to search German prisoners when they were captured. There was always a chance of finding important documents, especially on officers, and it was also important to establish that the prisoners had no weapons. There was always a suspicion of treachery on the part of German prisoners. There were a number of reports of attacks made by men after they had surrendered. One prisoner was reported to have had a bomb under his hat, which he used to murder his captor after he had surrendered.

In May the *Monthly Record Magazine* of the British Empire Union had some interesting comments on the Germans. Rudyard Kipling, who was one of Masterman's propaganda writers, wrote that 'there are two races in the world, Germans and human beings'. The magazine also gave the numbers of crimes committed in Germany compared with Britain over the previous century. These included incest (Germany 573, Britain fifty-six) and unnatural crimes (Germany 841, Britain 290). The magazine also included a list of hospital ships sunk by German U-boats and how when the Germans left Noyon they took fifty young French girls to act as officer's servants. They also described how they had cut down fruit trees and thrown filth into wells. Mr H. Tomlinson of the *Daily News* said that he could not picture the Germans being received back into the European family after the war. The anti-German feeling that was still evident in the country resulted in rumours about the men working on farms around the Handforth camp. The commandant of the camp Lieutenant Colonel T. Dauncey said that prisoners were being accused of gouging the eyes out of potatoes before they planted then to stop them growing. Dauncey said that all the men sent out from the camp were volunteers. They were mostly farmers themselves who longed for the open-air work they could do on the farms. They also ploughed, milked, dug, and spread manure. He asked if they would risk being sent back to the monotony of the prison for breaking a few shoots of potatoes, which would soon grow back anyway. There were some disturbances at the Stratford camp in May. The prisoners in the camp included German, Austrians, and some Poles and there was said to be bad feeling between the Germans and the others. A report in the local newspaper in May said how a Polish prisoner had hit a German while holding a razor, which cut his face. The Pole had just finished shaving and claimed that he had forgotten he held the razor. By the time the case came to court the accused's nationality had changed to Hungarian. The headline in the newspaper said 'German bully cut with razor'. The charges were dismissed.

The number of air raids taking place put a severe strain on the population and after one heavy raid in June the King was quickly on the scene to visit the victims of the raid in a number of London hospitals. No doubt this did much to raise moral amongst the public who were still very patriotic towards the Royal family, despite their German connections.

By the end of June there were a number of internees being employed by farmers. Many had been reluctant at first to use the men, but of the first units released to work there had been no escapes and none of them had to be returned to camps for any reason. Where a number of workers were living on a farm this was then classed as a camp. The use of aliens as workers was a step forward. Some had found that employment was not open to them before internment. Fritz Schrieber had been the managing director of Tennents Brewery, Glasgow. He along with other Germans had been responsible for the introduction of larger brewing in Scotland. When he left his employment at the brewery he was told that it would not be in the interest of the company to re-employ foreigners in the future. It was not only employers who were against employing enemy aliens. There had been cases where British workers had threatened to strike because the company they worked for employed Germans. In some cases the German workers were then dismissed in the interests of keeping the native workers happy.

There was a clear example of how the actions of one man could make such a difference to the conditions in a camp in May. The camp at Stratford, east London, had supposedly been a transit camp and had been open early in the war, but it was only now about to close. The commandant at Stratford and his staff were to take over at Alexandra Palace, as the commandant there had been ill for some time. The commandant from Stratford had a bad reputation amongst internees as did one of his staff, Sergeant Trinneman. The new commandant had also previously been a governor in a Dublin prison who reportedly treated internees as convicts. When he arrived at Alexandra Palace he seemed quite polite to Rudolf Rocker, but did not seem to be very intelligent. Although it seems that the camp in Carpenter's Road, Stratford, closed sometime in 1917, according to Rudolf Rocker it was not the last that the town was to see of prisoners of war. A boy of about ten years old was woken by his father in the middle of the night sometime in 1917; he saw a long line of German soldiers lined up in the road outside his house. They were guarded by soldiers with fixed bayonets. The boy described the Germans as still covered in mud as if they had just arrived from France. Some of them were wearing spiked helmets. They marched away along Romford Road to Water Lane where two old houses had been turned into a camp. The houses were next to Water Lane School and the children at the school could see the prisoners in the garden.

In June there was an unusual complaint by the German government through the Swiss Minister in London. It was related to an article published in *The Daily Mirror* in January. The article claimed that a skeleton being used in anatomy class had been a live Hun twelve months before. The Germans claimed that the soldiers of their country deserved a decent burial and that in Germany they only used the skeletons of criminals for such purposes. The reply from the Foreign Office claimed that the skeleton in question was not from a dead German and that the *Mirror* had in fact printed a retraction in a following edition. The skeleton had been purchased by the National Institute for the Blind before August 1914. The government claimed that the bodies of German prisoners were always buried in a manner that is in accord of civilised people. Whether the living were treated with as much respect as the dead is debatable; many of the interned men found the lack of privacy in camps was one of the biggest problems they faced. There was also some trouble between the pro-British and the pro-German internees in the camps. The fact that so many of the internees after their internment were still pro-British is a surprise.

The majority of the interned aliens were men who had either come to Britain themselves or with their fathers who had done so to improve their lives or to escape military service and the military character of German life. They saw England as a land of justice and freedom and saw their imprisonment as an injustice. Many of those who had once been sympathetic towards England must have changed their attitude after years of confinement.

When Morgan's book *German Atrocities* was published in 1916 he made every effort to make sure that the reports of the atrocities were seen as true. He tried to find proof for the rumours of the crucifixion of a Canadian officer, which had been widespread earlier in the war and had been partly responsible for riots. At Canadian headquarters, near Ypres, Morgan found that the story of two officers being crucified by Germans was common knowledge among Canadian soldiers. Not surprisingly he failed to find any eyewitnesses to this event. He showed how strictly he adhered to the truth by stating that he was not including this report as proof of a German atrocity in which case he had no need to have mentioned it. He then went on to say that it is conceivable that those who had seen this incident it had perished and their testimony with them. He seems to be saying that the event may not have happened, though also stating that witnesses to the event had probably died—leaving the idea fresh in the readers mind that if there had been witnesses then it must have happened. If he was not going to use the supposed incident as proof of an atrocity then why mention it in his book. Morgan was very good at establishing the certainty of an incident in the readers mind without having any actual proof. He included the story of a member of a Highland Regiment who found himself in hospital with a Prussian. The Scotsman attacked the Prussian swearing that he had seen him bayonet a wounded British soldier as he lay helpless on the ground. Morgan went on to say that no action was taken as all Prussian guardsmen look the same, but had to add that despite a lack of corroboration of identity he was certain that the event had taken place. Many of the cases included in the book have similar levels of proof, which are Morgan's certainty—based on no evidence at all.

There was a great deal of interest from war correspondents in relation to the prisoners taken at the Battle of Messines in June. Percival Phillips described them as 'of all ages and sizes as they were marshalled into cages behind the front by their own NCO's under the control of a British Sergeant'. They showed a strict adherence to orders.

He described them as 'having the usual proportion of spectacled clerks, peasants, elderly artisans, and young boys'. Another correspondent, Phillip Gibbs, described where the prisoners were from and what this meant. There were Bavarians, Prussians, and Wartembergers. It was the Bavarians who had seemed to suffer the most under the British bombardment. He described the Wartembergers as next to the Saxons as 'the least savage and brutal of our foes'.

There had been none of the expected problems with the new commandant at Alexandra Palace until the end of June. The internees refused to accept a supply of herrings that were not fit to eat. The commandant called their actions rank insubordination. He ordered them to take the fish and eat it. His argument was that the government had sent the food so that it must be good enough to eat. Sargent Trinneman then introduced searches during visits, which had been stopped some time before. The wives of the internees were very intimidated by this and anyone trying to smuggle in chocolate or a cake for their husband was sent home with no visit. There was a strong feeling of discontent in the camp, but the commandant then reversed the restrictions the sergeant had put in place. Rudolf Rocker said that the commandant feared there being an outbreak of unrest at the camp so soon after he had taken over when there had been peace for so long.

Royal visits to hospitals were quite common during the war and no doubt did much to raise moral, especially after air raids. When Princess Mary visited Queen Mary's Naval Hospital, at Southend in July however, security was high on the agenda. The princess travelled from London into Essex by train and the train was followed by an aircraft, no doubt due to the number of air raids the town had suffered so far in the war.

Although there had been no policy of interning women, some were being held in internment camps; these were women who were suspected of spying. One of these disputed the right of the government to hold her through the courts in July. Hilda Howsain was being held in Aylesbury Internment Camp under the Defence of the Realm Act. Howsain was not an alien or of hostile association. She claimed to hate the system of government in Germany and before her arrest had worked as a nurse in Red Cross Hospitals. She had visited a man in Lausanne in Switzerland and had passed a message from him to a woman in England. It was later revealed that this woman was suspected of being a spy and of being involved in an assassination plot. The court argued that the government were entitled to deal with cases of espionage. If Parliament passed legislation and put the power into the hands of an official of the state to deal with such cases then the courts would be going outside their jurisdiction in saying that those powers were too wide. The lady had been interned under temporary and exceptional legislation for the term of the war.

The Swiss Legation visited the London County Asylum at Colney Hatch in July. Of the 3,000 patients forty-four were civilian internees from various camps. They were sufferers from Barbed Wire Disease or as they called it in the camps, Camp Vogel. The internees were not kept separate from the British patients in the asylum, but were spread amongst them.

Although a large number of British prisoners were interned in Holland the Dutch people were not all in favour of the British. There had been complaints that the Dutch people were short of potatoes, but that potatoes were still being sent to Britain. There were riots and attacks taking place on the lighters taking the vegetables to Britain. A British vessel had been attacked in Rotterdam by Dutch women who had carried off forty bags of potatoes. The Dutch police had done little to stop this happening. It appears that the problems of the Dutch people were of little consequence to the British Government as during a meeting of the war cabinet in July they were more concerned that Holland was exporting potatoes to Germany. They claimed this was in breach of an agreement, which stated that similar amounts would be offered to Britain. The Dutch government claimed that they had offered similar amounts, an offer, which was not taken up. While this dispute was taking place the opinion of the Dutch people seemed to be strongly anti-British and in early July there were serious riots in Amsterdam when crowds looted a quantity of potatoes that were awaiting shipment to Britain. This time the police did take sterner action and, along with support from troops, shots were fired on the rioters. There were further problems between Dutch fishermen and the British due to extended mining of the seas, which restricted Dutch shipping.

In July an air raid on London, in which fifty-seven people died, led to another outbreak of rioting. This took place in the east end and other parts of London such as Clerkenwell and Chelsea. It must have been more difficult to find enemy aliens to attack as so many had been interned by this time. It also did not seem to occur to those involved that the aliens who were living in the areas that rioting took place in were just as liable to be hurt in the raids as they were.

It was strange that Germany was often criticised as being a country where the people had no freedom while England was seen as the land of the free where people were allowed to believe and think what they wanted. There had obviously been a number of restrictions of the freedoms that had been enjoyed before the war. Free speech was one area that could still be enjoyed without official sanction. Because of this, pacifist meetings were still allowed and were even protected by the police. Although lawful, such meetings were not allowed to be held by sections of the British public. In July, when a pacifist meeting was held in London, the venue was kept secret to try and avoid trouble. Although, news had leaked out that the meeting would be held at the Brotherhood Church, Southgate Road, Kingsland. The church was surrounded by police officers, on foot and mounted, as well as a force of specials. A rival demonstration including a number of soldiers waving Union Jacks appeared at the church during the afternoon. The police were unable to stop them breaking into the church where the pacifist meeting immediately ended. The mob went on to wreck the church, smashing all the windows and pulling water pipes from the wall so that the church was flooded. As the pacifists left the church many were attacked and injured.

There is little doubt that if such an event took place in Germany it would have had widespread press coverage and been held up as an example of a government that treated its people with no respect or that allowed them any freedom. *The Times* mentioned the event and stated that many of the men who were involved in the pacifist meeting were bearded foreign types. It also described the men who fought back against a threatening mob as fighting pacifists, mentioning how one of the pacifist delegates was battered by four Australian soldiers. There was little doubt where the sympathy of the newspaper lay. Also mentioned was a similar event in Newcastle, which was also broken up by colonial soldiers.

Justus Heinz was taken prisoner at Langemark by the Irish Guards in July and was sent to England. The first camp he was sent to was at Costerdale in Yorkshire. Heinz was to spend the rest of the war attempting to escape and did so on a number of occasions. At Costerdale he tried getting through the barbed wire on a regular basis and was also a member of a group digging a tunnel, which was discovered just as it was about to be completed. Heinz then had a better idea—he would just walk out of the gate. It was not quite that easy, but he did it by disguising himself as the camp canteen manager

Mr Budd. Heinz had noticed that the guards on the gates had never asked Budd for a pass as they knew him so well. There was a second part to his plan as he had been told that all men booking a rail ticket had to show a pass so he would travel disguised as a woman. Despite the strict censoring of letters to and from POWs in Britain, Heinz claimed that the prisoners often used private codes in letters and he managed to ask his mother to send him all the items he needed from Germany. He claimed to have received a wig disguised as tobacco, and jewellery hidden in marmalade, jam, or even baked in a cake. He was also sent a quilt with women's clothing sewn inside it. There was women's clothing in the camp for use in theatricals, but Heinz claimed that the prisoners were under their word of honour not to use it for any other reason. Heinz walked to the gate disguised as Mr Budd and was let through with no problem. The real Mr Budd had been delayed by an accomplice of his. Heinz left at 7.50 p.m. As the sentries changed at 8 p.m. and Budd would leave after this there would be no way of their knowing that he had left twice. After a short distance Heinz changed into his woman's clothes. Shortly after he was approached by three soldiers who he guessed had come from the camp. The men recognised the bag he was carrying and Heinz realised that the game was up. The sentry change had been late so that they had seen two Mr Budd's leaving the camp. The whole escape attempt was treated as a joke, with Heinz claiming that the officers at the camp had laughed when they saw him dressed as a woman. I got the impression from reading of Heinz's escapades that he treated his numerous escape attempts in the same way. He was eventually sentenced to thirty-five days in Chelmsford Prison.

The *War Illustrated* published an article in July that claimed that there were many people profiting from the effects of the U-boats by charging high prices for goods. The article included a quote from a Cardiff coal owner who said that if he could get 40s a ton for coal from Sweden then he would not sell his coal for less to the people of London. This was because the government had introduced the Coal Price Limitation Act in July 1915 and it showed how government policy did not always work in the way it was expected to. In 1916 the average price of coal had been just over 16s a ton, but this government price limit only applied to coal prices at home. It was better for coal owners to sell their coal abroad for higher prices, which then led to shortages at home. This does seem unpatriotic when people at home were short of coal and yet it was still being exported for higher profits. It was also seen as another reason to have a grievance against German prisoners and internees who were also supplied with coal while many Britain's went without. It was not only coal that offered the opportunity for higher profits during wartime. The British and Argentine Meat Company handled meat from America to sell in England. In 1914 they had made a profit of £67,000 and by 1916 their profits had risen to £411,000. There were times when plenty of meat arrived in the country and this was then held by the suppliers in cold storage so as to keep the prices high as they were in the periods when there were shortages. According to *The Illustrated War News* the profits of this company were affected by the arrival of cheap meat from South Africa for a time, but then the prices for this meat also began to rise. The article went on to claim that one butcher was selling meat to a hotel that placed large orders at just over 11*d* a pound. At the same time the price of meat on sale in his shop to the general public was for the same meat 1*s* and 8*d*. If he was making a profit on the hotel price then he was making a much higher profit on the shop price. There may have been some of the population who suspected that those in command of supplies of food and coal were profiteering from the war and the U-boat menace. Though it was a much more obvious choice to blame those being held prisoners for using so much of the available supplies and to blame them for high prices and shortages, despite the fact that the majority of those interned were there because of the public opinion that wanted them interned in the first place.

There was often a lack of understanding between the guards and the prisoners in the camps. When a man escaped from Alexandra Palace the commandant abused the company captain for not telling them immediately about the escape. The captain did not see it as part of his duty to act as a policeman in the camp, but to attend to internal administration. In a conversation with Major Mott, Rudolf Rocker said that he agreed with the captain in that he was not a policeman. Mott asked him if he thought that interned men had the right to try and escape. Rocker pointed out that two Englishmen had escaped from the German internment camp at Ruheleben and had been praised for it in the British press for doing so.

In August Lord Newton reported back on the Prisoner of War Conference that had taken place at The Hague. The exchange of civilians was to resume as well as that of incapacitated combatants. There was to be a quicker notification of the names of those captured and all new prisoners would be allowed to contact their families straight away. There was an offer from Holland to provide places for 16,000 prisoners in their country and there were also many in Switzerland. This offer was to include 7,500 invalid combatants, 6,500 officers and NCO's who had been prisoners for eighteen months, and 2,000 civilian invalids. There had to be a comment from the German delegate General Frederick that the treatment of German prisoners in this country was superior to that in any other. The Hague Conference had been seen as unusual by many in that enemies would meet to discuss events while they were still at war. The reason for the eighteen month rule was that a Doctor A. L. Vischer had studied men in camps on the Isle of Man and had noticed mental problems in long-term inmates that he called Barbed Wire Psychosis, which involved loss of memory and irritability. Men would often talk to themselves and become suspicious of other inmates. It was less prevalent among those who worked, including those who used the camp workshops to make things. The agreement included a more lenient schedule of disabilities for those to be repatriated. All punishments inflicted on combatants and civilian prisoners for offences before 1 August 1917 were to be remitted. Reprisals against prisoners of war only to be carried out after four weeks' notice was one of the points agreed, but there was also another that stated that all reprisals against British prisoners for sentences passed on Germans who had attempted to escape to be cancelled at once. Punishment for trying to escape was to be limited to fourteen days or two months in cases of aggravated escapes. No prisoner repatriated was to be used at the front or on lines of communication. It was agreed that all prisoners who have been in captivity for at least eighteen months and who were suffering from Barbed Wire Disease shall in the future be recognised as suitable for internment in Switzerland and other neutral countries. If after being there three months there was no considerable improvement in health then their problems would be treated as serious and they should be considered for repatriation.

The support for the war in Britain shown by the constant use of mobs to break up any anti-war or pacifist meetings was not shared by all those in the colonies. There has always been a view that men from many of the countries of the empire rushed to enlist and fight in the war for Britain. In August in Montreal, Canada, this was far from the case. The Conscription Bill was introduced to Canada and a crowd of around 5,000 gathered in Montreal and pledged to resist conscription to the death. There were threats to shoot Sir Robert Borden, the Canadian prime minister. Shots were fired by the mob and it was very difficult for the police to break up the meeting. There was a great deal of damage done with windows being smashed and several arrests were made.

Living with internment was very difficult for those who were being held. The men in the camps could see the outside world and life going on without them through the wire, with many of the men in a panic over losing their reason. A large number of interned men were removed to asylums. After the third Christmas in the camps, a report by the Society of Friends was sent to the Prime Minister asking if some other method could not be used in dealing with aliens due to the poor mental condition of many of those interned. The introduction of workshops, where prisoners could produce items to sell, was seen as a useful aid to the prisoner's welfare. It was noted that many men interned for more than six months had some mental problems. It was found in the Isle of Man that no prisoners who used the workshops had to go to an asylum. The workshops were a viable alternative to paid work, which was not available to all. Creating things did not only help pass the time, but was a way of keeping sane.

There were some interesting prisoners captured during August. New Zealanders near Messines captured a number of very young German soldiers. It seems that it was not unusual to find teenagers amongst the enemy ranks. There was also a Hanoverian prisoner who had an arm band with Gibraltar written on it. This showed that his regiment had been part of George III's Army and helped to defend Gibraltar during the great siege against the Spanish and French in the American War of Independence.

The end of August was to see a number of German prisoners at large in the country. Six of them were from the Stobs internment camp and included two members of a zeppelin crew. Another man had escaped from Oldcastle camp. Two were also missing from the Handforth Camp. Large numbers of escaped German soldiers roaming the countryside must have been a worry for the public. One of the men at large had caused some disquiet about prisoners being allowed out to work. Benno Liipchutz had been interned at the Douglas Camp and had been part of a work party at a brush factory. He escaped as the prisoners were being mustered to return to the camp. There was also a worry that sending small parties of prisoners out to work may have left them open to attacks from the public during spells of anti-German feeling.

The war correspondent Basil Clarke visited a prison camp close to the front in France in August and wrote an article for the *War Illustrated* about the conditions. A road made from logs led to the camp, which had a double barbed wire fence enclosing an area of around 3 acres. There was a space of about 10 yards between the two fences where British sentries patrolled. There were also towers at each corner from where the sentries could watch the fences. The guards were garrison duty men of around forty years of age and were commanded by a major. The guards had wooden huts to live in along with a kitchen and a recreation hut, while the major had an office, warmed by an American-type stove. The guards numbered about forty men, which seemed to be many more than the number of prisoners in the camp at the time Clarke arrived. The rest of the prisoners were out repairing roads about 1 mile from the camp. When they returned to camp they were commanded by their own *Feldwebel* (the equivalent of a British sergeant major), though they were guarded by British soldiers. The prisoners slept in tents that were within the fences. Many of the prisoners wore British Army boots and overcoats and the major explained that they were given to men who did not have suitable ones of their own. The prisoners walked into the camp in columns of two and were kept in line by the commands of the *Feldwebel*. Clarke claims that when one man stepped out of line the *Feldwebel* struck him in the side of the head, knocking him to the ground. None of the other prisoners or guards seemed surprised by this. Clarke was curious to know what the German soldiers were treated like in the trenches, if this was how they were treated in prison camps. It became apparent as to why British prisoners were treated poorly by the Germans, if this was how they were treating their own men.

The number of prisoners at large in Britain grew again towards the end of the month when two German airmen escaped from Holyport Camp. It was believed that they would try and steal an aircraft to get back to Germany; perhaps this was why so many airman attempted to escape; they may have had a chance of getting back to Germany by aircraft, although it may also have been that airmen were more daring than infantrymen. Two more German officers then escaped from Sandhill Park with another escaping from Knockaloe, making the number at large sixteen. The man who had escaped from Oldcastle camp had by this time been recaptured. One French camp had a novel way of deterring prisoners from escaping. All the French prisoners worked during the day, but at night they had to surrender their boots, which were then guarded all night by a sentry. Another camp made the prisoners surrender their belts or braces at night.

There had been suspicions for some time that the more distinguished and well connected an alien was the less chance that there was of him being interned. This was shown to be untrue in September when Mr Phillip Alexus Laszlo de Lombos was ordered to be interned. Unfortunately, when there was an attempt to arrest him at his London home, it was found that he had been on his customary holiday in the countryside since July and was not yet expected back. Mr Laszlo de Lombos had been a well-known figure in London society for many years. Born in Budapest, he had come to England and married the sixth daughter of Mr H. Guinness of Burton Hall Dublin and had five sons. He had become a well-known court painter and as well as his house at Palace Gate he also had a studio in Camden Hill Road. He had won awards for painting the portraits for many of the royal families of Europe including Edward VII, Pope Leo XIII, and the Kaiser.

Although the country was seemingly gripped with widespread hatred of Germans there were still some who had a level of sympathy for them. This was mainly towards military prisoners, judging by the number of people who were charged with either fraternising or supplying them with gifts. In September a young boy, Albert Althus who was sixteen and worked on canal boats at Manchester, was charged with giving cigarettes to German prisoners. This happened at Leigh Camp when Private J. Wood was on guard duty near the canal bank and heard the prisoners speaking to someone. He saw the boy who admitted that he had been throwing cigarettes over the fence to the prisoners. He was then arrested as nothing was allowed to be given to the prisoners without being examined first and was remanded in custody.

The internees at Ruhleben were mainly civilians, so escape attempts were not a common occurrence, though one did manage it; this was Mr A. E. Keith who had been living in Neuss, Germany, for a year before the war. He was interned, but tried to escape on a number of occasions. The first was from a sanatorium, which invalids from Ruhleben could be taken to if they could afford it. He managed to reach the Dutch border before being arrested. Mr Keith was locked in an official building and broke a hole in the roof trying to get out, but was captured again. As a punishment he was sent to a prison in Berlin. This time he escaped with another prisoner, Wallace Ellison, who later wrote the book *Escapes and Adventures*. They were captured again near the border. This time in prison, Mr Keith heard about a swamp near the Dutch border that was supposedly impassable and would therefore not be well guarded. He was then sent back to Ruhleben. It was easy to get out of the camp by crawling under the wire, which was what Keith did along with some other prisoners. They covered some of the distance to the border by train and the rest by walking at night. They managed to cross the swamp and eventually believed that they were in Holland. They saw a house and thought that it must not be in Germany as there was a bowl of potatoes on the table. After arriving in London Mr Keith received a telephone call from Wallace Ellison who had also escaped.

Justus Heinz who had escaped from Costerdale and been recaptured dressed as a woman was sent to Holyport camp on his release from Chelmsford prison. He described this as the best camp he had been in for personal comfort, though this did not stop him from trying to escape again. In one attempt he was caught in the middle of the barbed wire. Heinz was later transferred along with forty-nine other officers to a camp near Wakefield. He said that when the order had come through to transfer fifty men the commandant had taken the opportunity to get rid of the most troublesome of the prisoners in the camp, which included him. Heinz used the opportunity to stage another escape and jumped off the train that was taking him to the new camp. He got off just after the train passed South Elmshall Station—the clothes he was wearing could pass as civilian dress—from there he walked to Doncaster and took a train to London. From the details of his story it was amazing how easy it was for an escaped prisoner to travel around the country. In London, Heinz found that Trafalgar Square had been turned into a devastated French Village, no doubt for some collection for the Red Cross. He spent a number of evenings at the theatre and managed to book into a hotel posing as a Frenchman—without showing any identification. Heinz travelled by train to Cardiff where he hoped to stow away aboard a ship. He claimed that he read about his previous escape in a newspaper with the headline 'Masquerading Hun Officer in a Woman's Dress'. Scotland Yard believed that he was again dressed as a woman. Heinz had hoped to get aboard a Spanish ship, but instead got Spanish Flu and had to give himself up because he was so ill. He was sent to Lofthouse Park camp until he was recovered and then to spend a further fifty-six days in Chelmsford Prison.

September saw the arrival of 450 wounded British prisoners returning to London via Switzerland. Some of the men had been prisoners since early in the war. They had been told while in captivity in Germany that London had been bombed out of existence and that Gibraltar and India had fallen.

Although the majority of German prisoners in Britain did not work for the first years of the war it was permissible to employ them in public works at fixed rates of pay. One job that was given to prisoners was to help build their own camps. This could also include cutting down the trees to provide the timber for huts and making roads to the camps. It was claimed that British prisoners in German hands were often forced to dig trenches in front line areas or work in unhealthy mines.

Often problems occurred in internment camps when officers acted off their own bat without following the camp rules. A new censor arrived at Alexandra Palace and one of his first acts was to stop a parcel of books for Rudolf Rocker because they were Socialist titles. When Rocker planned to appeal to the commandant the censor backed down and he was given the books. The new censor then confiscated another prisoner's copy of a book that he claimed was immoral. The man appealed to the commandant and it was returned. The censor then tried to stop one of Rockers lectures as he claimed that it was on modern-German literature, which was not allowed. This was because lectures on modern-English literature had been banned in Germany. The commandant called Rocker to his office who told him that the subject of the lecture, Hoffman, had died in 1822. The lecture then went ahead. The censor appeared to be a power-hungry man or one who thought that everyone should live in his image. The threat of being sent to the Isle of Man was one that those with families in London constantly feared, though men with wives in London were normally spared being sent there (although some had to, due to new internees arriving at the Palace). The censor was responsible for sending men away without any regard to their family position; in some cases the wives of men arrived at the Palace only to find their husbands had been sent to the Isle of Man.

There were serious problems concerning food by this point in the war, but this was not always to do with shortages, although sugar and butter were scarce. There was still food available at a price; some butchers in the better-off parts of London were charging prices for meat that had trebled since before the war. At Knockaloe it was said that the prisoners were eating dogs, cats, and seagulls to bolster their rations. I'm not sure where the dogs and cats came from as I doubt that they were allowed to keep pets in the camp. To help with food production any land not being used was taken over by the government. The commissioner of the Board of Agriculture and Fisheries inspected a derelict farm near Cambridge. The 400-acre Glebe Farm at Little Grandsden was taken over and twenty soldiers were put to work there to clear the overgrown land. It was planned to establish a prisoner of war camp on the farm—the prisoners would live in tents during the summer and work on the farm.

In another event at Knockaloe, John Kelly, a civilian employed at the camp, was sentenced to three months imprisonment for giving a bottle of whiskey to a German prisoner at the camp. Kelly worked on the light railway leading to the camp and left the whiskey in a shed to be picked up by a prisoner who was also working on the railway.

Things were not going well in Germany and there was an event that must have shocked the German government in August when 400 German sailors from the battleship *Prinzeregent Luitpold* marched into the town at Wilhelmshaven calling for an end to the war; the men later returned to their ship and the ringleaders were executed.

There was a report in *The Times* at the end of August as to the numbers of enemy prisoners captured since the Battle of Arras in April. They were 46,155 taken by the British, 43,723 by the French, 40,681 (mainly Austrians) by the Italians, and 37,221 by the Russians. Up until this time it was the other allies who took the most prisoners. The total number captured by the British since the war began was now 102,218. The total number of British and Indian prisoners captured by the Germans since the war began was 43,000.

The escapes continued to mount into September although the two airmen from Holyport had been recaptured before they could steal an aircraft. Seven men, six sailors, and one soldier escaped from Pattishall Camp. Their names and descriptions were given in the report of their escape, but how the men escaped was rarely mentioned in the newspapers.

Although there had been complaints of prisoners being held near the front it was obvious that any held in France could be at risk. In early September, during an air raid on what was described as an inland town in France, a number of German prisoners were being moved. The enemy airmen must have believed that the men were British troops and dropped a number of bombs on them killing forty-one of the prisoners.

There was a report of how a prisoners escaped in mid-September. He was being moved from one camp to another by train and was on the 4.05 p.m. from Woking. As it slowed at Walton-on-Thames the prisoner evaded his escort, opened the door and jumped out of the carriage. He then disappeared into Ashley Wood.

With rationing affecting the population as a whole, there was obviously great interest in any irregularities concerning internees and their rations. In October a case was heard at Middlesex session regarding John Immer, a kitchen superintendent at Alexandra Palace Camp, and Hector Davis, a greengrocer of Muswell Hill who was a contractor to the camp. Immer claimed that the rice allowed for his men was often issued in bulk instead of as the daily ration of 250lb. He then gave all of the men at the camp a portion of the rice, but was still left with 234 lb of rice, which he gave to Davis. According to the police there had been a number of irregularities between Davis and the prisoners with prohibited items such as eggs, bacon, butter, and even whiskey being supplied to the camp. The report in *The Times* emphasised the rationing effects on the population by stating that while the inhabitants of Muswell Hill could not get a potato at any price, large quantities were reaching the German prisoners through Davis. Both men were sentenced to twelve months hard labour. The feeling in the camp was that the problems had been due to Sergeant Trinneman and that under the previous commandant it would have been sorted out without the police being involved. Rudolf Rocker believed that the press had exaggerated the problem and that there were not any serious problems and that the incident happened just as the men had explained it. It was not only shortage of food that depressed the internees, one man found out that his four sons had all been killed in battle and the man's wife had gone mad at the news and was in an asylum. One can only wonder at how a man deals with such news, especially when interned away from his wife and family at such a sad time. As internment continued, there were still mistakes being made as to who was interned. Once confined in a camp it was difficult to get out again. In Alexandra Palace there was an Argentinian who was held for four months, a Dutchman held for five months, and a Russian held for seven months. There was even an Englishman who had been on his way back from America who did not have the correct papers so he was interned.

Many of the escaped prisoners often spent their days of freedom living rough and going hungry. One man, Lieutenant Paul Schumann, had a bit more style. He escaped from Chippenham Camp and booked into a hotel in London the following day. He aroused suspicion by writing the door number of his supposed address after the street name instead of before it as Germans do. The owner of the hotel went to the police and despite claiming to be Swiss Schumann was arrested.

The Illustrated War News reported on how German prisoners were being allowed to work outside the camps by this time. The report stated that the prisoners worked well, but only on the word of command and not on their own initiative. The men were paid and given extra rations for those involved in manual labour.

According to the war correspondent Perry Robinson it was no longer geography that was a measure of success in the war. It was the number of prisoners being taken. He claimed that 60,000 had been taken by the British in 1917. He wrote that the officers that had been captured were aware of the naval mutiny that had taken place in Germany and that similar feelings were being displayed in the Army.

There was an article published in the *New York Times Current History Magazine* in late 1917 written by Lord Northcliffe. Northcliffe had been a great advocate of internment in his newspaper, the *Daily Mail*, but this article was concerning his trip to the front in France. In the article he said that at home the authorities hid German prisoners while in France they were put to work. It would be difficult to realise that middle-aged men with pipes and young men with cigarettes were prisoners if it were not for the P. G. on their coats, which stood for prisoner de guerre. Northcliffe went on to mention large war schools where young conscripts from England were taught about war by officers who had been at the front. At one school Northcliffe saw a number of German prisoners on their way to their camp. He claimed that the prisoners were amazed at so many young troops arriving as they believed that England had run out of men. The prisoners were given excellent food and had plenty of tobacco. Although they were in a terrible condition when they arrived they were by then as well off as the British soldiers arriving from England.

The bad feeling at Alexandra Palace came to a head at the end of October when Sergeant Trinneman was accused of assault on an internee. He had not only assaulted the man, but had locked him in a cell. Many of the men refused to line up for the count as a result; though Major Mott released the man and the men eventually lined up. It was claimed by the internees that as the wife of one of them (Mueller) was leaving Trinneman rushed up to her swearing and telling her to leave; he then swore at Mueller who had protested. Mueller was then allegedly grabbed by the sergeant and another soldier and thrown into a cell. The sergeant ripped the man's coat off and threatened to rip his skin off as well. Mueller was sent to a court martial over the incident. Trinneman denied everything even after the soldier who had helped him told the truth. Mueller was acquitted and released. The commandant called the three battalion leaders in for a lecture about undermining discipline in the camp. They argued that it was Trinneman who was doing this not them. The sergeant eventually left the camp as it was clear to everyone that he was causing a problem. Rocker claimed that it was not only the internees that were glad to see the back of him, but the other guards and the officers as well.

By November the use of prisoners as labour on farms was spreading. Although many had been against it at first, the idea of these men being used to produce food for the country instead of sitting in camps and consuming it was seen to make sense and more employers began to come forward for the use of prisoners. Using prisoners would seem a good idea when there was such a shortage of men due to enlistment in the forces.

December was to see growing queues outside shops, especially for meat. It was the poor who suffered most from this and workers. Women who worked did not have time to spend hours standing in queues. In Parliament it was said that the ministry of food had an anxious time recently and were faced with a serious deficiency in meat and fats. By the end of the year there was a plan in place to save food and expense related to German prisoners. Many of those taken in France were kept in France to help with the workload of the labour corps, instead of being sent to England. They were provided with food that was sent out to feed the British Army and guarded by the large number of soldiers already in the area. The Germans were controlled by their own NCO's who passed on orders given by British officers. Discipline was very good amongst them, the German soldiers respectfully obeyed their superiors. The prisoners were paid a small wage so that they could buy some luxuries from the canteens in the camps. None were employed within 18 miles of the front and many worked at the French ports where the goods from England arrived to be unloaded. The food situation was getting much worse by late 1917 and new rules were put in place. It became an offence to throw rice at a wedding, using starch in laundry work was restricted, and it became an offence to adopt and feed stray dogs—a man was even fined £50 for collecting crusts for pig food. In October bakers were allowed add potatoes to bread. The queues in poorer areas in the cold winter of 1917 were the breeding ground for complaints that the rich were not short of food and the demands for compulsory rationing grew. This was partly true as the better off could either send their servants to queue or could have their shopping delivered, as grocers would do this for good customers. Margarine was often very difficult to find. Some parts of the country began their own rationing schemes before the national systems came into being; one of the first was Birmingham. The shortages of food did have an effect in the camps in Britain and even those in Gentleman's camps suffered. There was no food for sale in the canteens and parcels from home and from Germany had stopped. The men in the camps grew weaker from lack of decent food. In Lofthouse Park there was even an escape attempt. A tunnel was dug, but after heavy rain a cow in a nearby field stood above it and it collapsed, trapping the animal in the hole. The situation in Germany was much worse than it was in Britain with rationing in place well before it happened here. Queues in Germany were longer and often began hours before shops even opened. Soup kitchens did a roaring trade and the lack of fuel, such as coal, was another serious problem. To help with fuel shortages schools were used for one set of pupils in the morning and those from another school in the afternoon so that one school building could close.

By late 1917, there had been improvements in other areas. Some single huts had been allowed in the camp. One of the things that many of the inmates found very difficult was that there was never any privacy. According to Paul Cohen-Portheim all those men locked up without women for so long should have led to cases of homosexual contact, but the lack of privacy made this difficult. He claimed that this did not happen.

In November, the Battle of Cambria was the first real success of the tank. Until then the new weapons had been used in totally unworkable ground conditions, such as in the mud of Ypres. The success of the tank led to large numbers of prisoners being taken again. As in other battles they helped to bring in the wounded from both sides.

The question of internment had by this time raised its head in America since they had entered the war. The *New York Times Current History Magazine* published an article on the subject in late 1917. The article stated that Britain had interned all German subjects at the outbreak of the war, which was not quite accurate. This would not have been practical in America due to the enormous number of Germans in the country. Those suspected of being spies had been arrested or were being watched, but the majority of prisoners held in America were the crews of German vessels seized in American ports when they entered the war. These were at held at Ellis Island. Like Britain, American prisoners of war were not forced to work. To prepare for more prisoners, three war prison barracks had been established at Fort Macpherson, Fort Oglethorpe, and Fort Douglas.

Censorship of letters, both arriving for prisoners and being sent by them to their families in Germany, was mainly carried out by women. There were often letters or items included in parcels that were banned and were kept in storage until the end of the war. Whether these were ever returned to their owners is not clear.

Two men escaped in October 1917, and were arrested in Manchester. Three other men escaped on a Friday—it was thought they had vaulted over the fence. They were caught on the following Monday asleep in a haystack near Ormskirk. These are not all the escapes or attempted escapes at the time as there were escapes from a number of camps.

The arrival of more prisoners at Leigh later in the war was greeted with more criticism. The men were described as a rabble who were not marching properly; they were weedy looking and poor specimens in comparison with British soldiers. Their condition shouldn't have been unexpected, as no doubt they had spent longer in the trenches than the earlier arrivals. There were also complaints that photography by the public was forbidden as the prisoners marched to the camp; this came as a shock to those not used to being restricted in any way, and was described in the local press as Prussian methods, which was what the country was fighting against. Further complaints were lodged because the prisoners' escorts changed the route that the prisoners took to the camp, apparently for no other reason than to prevent the locals from seeing them. This often resulted in the crowd rushing to viewpoints, which led to women and children being knocked over and hurt. The *Leigh Chronicle* criticised these methods, saying that unless the prisoners were brought in by aeroplane there was no way of stopping the locals from seeing them. Towards the end of 1917 prisoners from the camp at Leigh were allowed out of the camp to work. This included 200 men who worked at Partington Steel Works. They travelled there by tram, accompanied by armed guards, and were paid a penny an hour. No doubt the local newspaper would have had some negative views on this.

A shortage of workers on the land was a problem at the end of 1917, despite some help from soldiers, women, and even schoolboys. The situation was partly overcome by the use of some German prisoners, but this was still not widespread. Usually prisoners were released to work in large groups that could be guarded, but this was not appropriate for farm work. The scheme led to huts being erected on farms, so prisoners could live there and then did not have to be transported between camp and farm twice a day. For groups that did have to march to work and return to the camp there was a guard of three soldiers per group, and rations for the prisoners were supplied by the camp.

By the end of the year there was an even more severe effect of the war on the population. Shortages in many basics such as tea, meat, and margarine led to even more enormous queues at times. *The Times* reported one queue in London to be of 3,000 people and that after two hours 1,000 of them went away empty handed. Working long hours and queuing for so long was another factor in the unhappiness of the population—as they saw it, internees and POWs did not need to queue for their food.

5

1918

The final year of the conflict saw civil war in Russia and their withdrawal from the conflict against the Germans. The release of troops from the east led to a huge German advance on the western front. Another form of death began to affect the troops and the people at home as the Spanish Flu epidemic began to take hold. The Royal Flying Corps and the Royal Naval Air Service amalgamated to become the RAF.

The failure to defeat the Germans after so many years of war had led to a number of conspiracy theories, which had grown in stature throughout the conflict. One of these was the Hidden Hand theory whose proponents believed that Germany controlled Britain and prevented them from obtaining victory. This idea had in fact been prevalent before the war with such writers such as Ian Colvin (lead writer for the *Morning Post*) promoting it. Colvin actually claimed that Germany had controlled Britain for much of its history. A book had been published in the previous year called the *Hidden Hand* by Arnold White, which claimed that Downing Street and Fleet Street were controlled by Germany. This then developed into a new theory that claimed German spies were sexually corrupting major figures in Britain who would then be in their power due to blackmail. One of the sexual corruption theories main champions was Pemberton Billing. Billing was a member of parliament and was very right wing. He was strongly anti-homosexuality and believed that this form of sexual conduct was one of the means used to corrupt British politicians. Billing was later prosecuted for libel when he accused a dancer, Maud Allen, of being a lesbian. There was not only a book about this

German control theory, but also a play at the Middlesex Theatre in London that was also called the *Hidden Hand*. One of its customers was an escaped German POW, Justus Heinz. He found it thrilling, but described it as the most anti-German performance in the world. He described the atmosphere around him as not being very pro-German and wondered what would have happened if the audience had found out that there was a German officer sitting amongst them.

Perhaps one of the most surprising things about 1918 was that after four years of war there were still numerous disputes over enemy aliens. One would have thought that by this time the matter would have been settled to everyone's satisfaction. Of course, while the government still did not believe in across-the-board internment others did, and there were still constant calls for stricter enforcement of it by right wing politicians and their supporters. While internment had been going on for some time in England in other countries it was just about to begin. Now that America had entered the war they began to plan for the internment of aliens to guard against espionage, arson, and sabotage. The task in America was on a much larger scale with more than half a million unnaturalised Germans in the country.

There were some problems involving sick British prisoners who were to be sent to Switzerland at the beginning of 1918. The Swiss government had said that they were willing to accept prisoners with Tuberculosis, but wanted to know the numbers involved before they agreed. It seemed though that the Swiss medical commission that decided on which prisoners should be accepted were not visiting camps in Germany, but only inspecting prisoners selected by the Germans.

The failure to exchange prisoners of war was often blamed on the lack of agreement by the Germans. It seems that the British military were just as much to blame for the lack of movement. This was shown when Lord Lamington asked in the House of Lords in January whether the military authorities were still opposed to the exchange of prisoners of war. The government considered it worthwhile to suffer some military disadvantage to release some unfortunate officers and men from the hardships they were suffering in German hands; Earl Stanhope replying for the War Office said that this was the case. They had no objection to exchanges that led to prisoners being interned in neutral countries, but they were against the repatriation of prisoners. He said that the object of the war was to put out of action as many Germans as possible—every German sent back to Germany increased the power of that country; if large numbers were sent back then it would prolong the war. They could not trust Germany to agree not to use released prisoners in combat again, with some who had been released had already been involved in fighting again. There was also the problem of using ships to transfer prisoners when the vessels could be used to bring American troops over to Europe and to carry food and other supplies to Britain.

The poor opinions of foreigners in relation to the English was shown in a report in *The Times* on a coroner's inquest on fourteen people killed during an air raid in London on 28 January. The deaths were due to a stampede at an air raid shelter after maroon rockets were fired to warn of a raid. Air raid warnings took a number of methods in the war. The coroner said that the deaths were caused due to the panic, which was almost entirely displayed on the part of persons who might be called foreigners. He went on to say that one could have hoped that in London people would be by this time be able to retain their powers of self-confidence and control even during air raids. These were qualities that would have enabled them to act differently and not in a way unworthy of men, nearly approaching the ways of the lower animals. A police inspector said that the crowd, which consisted mainly of aliens, lost their head when they saw the rockets and rushed for the shelter. It then seems that some of the people dropped items that they were carrying and stopped to pick them up. They were then knocked over and others fell onto them, leading to the suffocation of several of the victims. The inspector was amazed at the number of able-bodied men who were involved and nearly all of them were of alien types. The inspector went on to say that he was proud that there had been no similar trouble with English people. The coroner went on to say that air raid shelters could cause a number of deaths in children who caught chills while in the shelters. He said that he went to bed during raids and if he was killed then he was ready to be laid out, which he obviously meant was the British way to act. There was also mention of the amount of money found on the victims, which again gave the impression that the aliens were rushing to the shelter to save their riches as well as their skins. On the same evening in London another shelter suffered a direct hit from a bomb and twenty-eight people died. In this case as there was no blame attached to the occupants of the shelter and there did not seem to be any comments in the media as to the nationality of the dead.

January eventually saw the beginning of rationing of other foods. This was partly due to signs of malnutrition that were appearing in the poorest members of the population. Sugar was the first item to be rationed, starting in London and then spreading across the country. Restrictions did not always work well. When certain foods had the price fixed they often disappeared from sale altogether. Some grocers would not sell sugar to people who were not registered with them unless they bought other items as well. The well-known muffin man with a tray of them on his head disappeared from the countries streets where he had been a common sight for so long. The food controller Lord Rhonda was a supporter of communal kitchens and personally opened one in Silvertown in the east end of London. Although these were opened in working-class areas it was not only the working class who used them. Lord Rhonda said at the time that compulsory rationing had to come, but that the people of Britain were in no way undergoing anything like the problems that the people of Germany had.

There had been talks going on for some time over the repatriation of some civilian internees. Many of those who were supposed to be sent home were moved to Alexandra Palace, but then as the negotiations became drawn out the camp was filled to overflowing. The rooms that had been used as schools had by this time become bedrooms; areas were now terribly crowded and much of what had been available as a way of passing the time was now at an end. Meanwhile German military prisoners were still escaping. Three men escaped from Water Lane Camp in Stratford in January after digging a tunnel that cut through tree roots in the garden. The men were captured a few days later by the sea at Walton-on-the-Naze and returned to the camp.

The end of January saw a notice appear in Alexandra Palace asking that anyone who thought they should go to Holland for medical reasons should put their name down for a medical examination. Conditions in Holland were said to be much better and the camp for civilians was at Hattem. It was said that those with money could even pay to stay in private homes rather than in a camp. The food was better and so was the level of freedom allowed to the internees.

The definition of who was a friendly or an enemy alien was still being decided and in February the government finally made the decision that Poles resident in Britain—who were technically of German or Austrian nationality, but whose sympathies lie with the Allies—could be treated as alien friends; this also applied to Russian Poles. How their sympathies were confirmed was not clear. Claiming to be pro-British may have been a way of avoiding internment, but were they always telling the truth.

With the population of the country now subject to rationing the same rules were applied to war prisoners. The meat ration for them was reduced from 30 oz to 20 oz. It was also pointed out that the general population could purchase substitutes for meat if they were available while those imprisoned could not. The reduction in rations for war prisoners led to complaints from Germany, as would be expected. This was regardless of the fact that it was due to the German U-boats sinking ships bringing food to the country that helped to lead to shortages.

The discussions over further prisoner exchanges continued and in February Lord Newton told the war cabinet that the exchange of interned civilians was impractical. He said that there were 15,000 Germans who would take the opportunity to return home if they could. However, this would be in exchange for only 3,000 British subjects. Therefore he wanted 5,000 British military prisoners included in the exchange who would be sent to Holland. The factors in favour of the exchange was that the collapse of Russia had already given the Germans larger numbers of men for use on other fronts so the release of the German civilians would not make much difference to the numbers of men they had available. The expense of keeping them and amount of food that the prisoners needed would be reduced. The small amount of work interned men did was minimal and would not be greatly missed. The facts against exchange were that the public would not have been happy about such an unbalanced exchange. There was not much chance of Germany agreeing to the inclusion of 5,000 military prisoners. They would also not count merchant seamen as civilians—many British merchant ships were by this time armed. Lord Newton therefore concluded that the exchange was not to the advantage of the state. The question of whether merchant seamen were civilians or combatants was a hotly disputed subject. German merchant seamen were treated as civilians in Britain, but British merchant seamen were not in Germany. Some British seamen had been involved in previous exchanges, but these were from unarmed merchant ships and fishermen.

The plans to exchange some internees for those held in Germany, and also to transfer some internees to neutral countries where the food supply was better, had begun to take place by this time. This happened with a number of internees from Lofthouse Park. The exchange process was a farce; when the men chosen arrived in Rotterdam they found they weren't expected. After some confusion those bound for

Germany were put aboard trains, while those bound for Holland were left on the dockside. It seems that internment in Holland was just confinement in the town itself, a sort of parole system, but there was no camp for the men. It was not possible for them to find their own quarters as they had no papers—not having been allowed to take any of their identification papers with them. The lack of an address also meant they were unable to get ration cards to buy food. There was obviously still confusion about the ways of proving identities. Paul Cohen-Portheim was one of those released internees who found himself in Rotterdam, and he asked his mother in Germany to send his birth certificate to the German legation in the town. When it arrived he was not allowed to claim it without proof of identity such as a birth certificate. After much argument the official opened the letter and handed him the certificate, which Cohen-Portheim handed back as proof of his identity; then he was allowed to take it. This enabled him to find somewhere to live and to get a ration card.

Many camp inmates found freedom hard to come to terms with when they were released. For so long they had only seen familiar faces in the camp that they found the strangers that now surrounded them was a worry. Other everyday things were also difficult to come to terms with, such as climbing stairs and sleeping on a floor above the ground. They also found it difficult to stay in a room for any length of time, having been so used to getting out of their huts as often as possible. The situation for Rudolf Rocker was slightly different. He had applied for internment in Holland at the end of February and had been passed as unfit and could therefore go. However, when the lists went up Rocker found that his name was on the one for those going to Germany. As he had always been in opposition to the Kaiser he expected to be thrown into prison if he returned to Germany. Although Rocker was glad to be out of the camp he was sad to leave England as it had been his home for so long. The men being transferred were first taken to an old workhouse at Spalding. Many of the other men there had come from the Isle of Man. From there they went to Boston. There they were searched again by a young officer who swore at them and broke open the cases of anyone not quick enough with to open it with their key. Anything new was confiscated as it was not allowed to be taken out of the country. The steamer they crossed to Holland in was the *Sindora*. It was comfortable and they were well treated by those on board. Rocker and the others bound for Germany were separated and locked in a room guarded by soldiers when they arrived in Holland.

They were then put on a train bound for Germany; Rocker tried to escape by jumping off the train, but was caught. When they arrived in Germany they were told of a number of regulations and given a meal that was as bad as what they had been given in the camp in England. The next morning each man had to say where he came from and send a telegram to a friend or family member in the area who would vouch for them. Rocker told the man in charge that he wanted to return to Holland because he had fled from Germany many years before. It seemed that Rocker was in just as bad a position as he had been in England. His details had to be sent to Berlin where someone would make the decision as to what to do with him. He was told that this could take up to a year and then he may find himself locked up in Germany instead of in England. He was billeted in a school building, but had to report to soldiers at the station twice a day.

By February it was impossible to find any veal in London and in the capital and the six Home Counties butter, margarine, and meat was now only available with ration cards. Even children at boarding schools had to have their own ration cards. Rationing then began to spread to the rest of the country. The lack of food and fuel for warming homes was one of the reasons why the influenza epidemic was doing such damage to the population weakened by poor food and cold housing.

There was another report of German prisoners being taken in the *War Illustrated* in March 1918. The report contained a number of photographs and, in keeping with most press reports, one image was described as showing that the flower of the Germany Army had either been killed or was wilting under Allied artillery fire, as the men were of a wretched physique. In one of the other images, however, it is mentioned how many of the men were very tall.

There were claims from Germany that the British government were housing German prisoners in areas that were liable to be bombed as a reprisal for the Germans putting British prisoners in a camp at Karlsruhe, which was also likely to be under attack from British and French bombs. Lord Newton claimed that it was understood that the reason for Germany using Karlsruhe was that it was because suitable accommodation was available there. It was the same reason that German prisoners were housed in areas likely to be bombed. Newton said that reprisals are not the exact word to use even if we are in fact following the German practice. There was nothing new in the presence of German prisoners being in areas that were subject to attack. There have been huge camps in London filled with German prisoners that have been likely to be the subject of air raids for some time.

Although there was no organised process of evacuation for those in areas under the threat of air raids some more localised movement did take place. One of these had occurred the previous year when a number of mothers with children had been invited to move from Poplar to spend a month in Maidenhead, which had so far been free from air raids. This was to cause an unexpected result for those towns further west. The kindness of the people of the Thameside town was repaid by what was described in *The Times* as an 'Invasion of Aliens'. News of the safety of places such as Maidenhead had obviously spread through the bombed east end. The town had suffered an influx of Russian Jews from the east end of London numbering up to 3,000 people. They took over all the empty properties and before rationing were buying all the food that was available in the town. Many local property owners had sold their premises to these newcomers who had then gone to court to evict the present tenants so that they could move in themselves. The men of these families still travelled to London each day to continue with their business and had season tickets on the railways. There were reports that season tickets would now be abandoned, but this would also affect those who had travelled into London for many years for employment. The same events were also occurring in Reading and other places to the west of London where large numbers of aliens were moving in. There were similar problems for Henley, although on a smaller scale; it was more of a problem to get to London by train from there than the towns closer to the capital or those on a direct rail line. The arrival of aliens was not entirely unwelcome. There were a number of houses in the town that had stood empty for years and these were quickly taken up for rent. The problem was that what food was still available for sale now had to go much further. There was a further report on Maidenhead in *The Times* at the end of March. There were a number of complaints over the aliens who had moved into the town, buying up much of the available meat. It was hoped that rationing would improve this situation—meat was to be added to the rationed foods from April. Some were worried that the influx would change the character of the town as a resort. However, local councillors said that press reports were exaggerated and that the aliens were orderly people and deserve sympathy for running away from dangers that the inhabitants of the town had not experienced themselves. The direct train line into London was obviously one of the main attractions for those wanting to get out of London due to the bombing. Slough, which had a direct line, was very full, leading to locals complaining that the land girls who came to work on farms in the area could find no accommodation. Places like Eton and Windsor, which had no direct train service, were less affected. The majority of the reports on the alien invasion of the Thameside towns concentrated on the disadvantages of the local population due to their arrival. In Slough it was said that the aliens who worked in London took advantage of the limited cheap workmen's tickets on the train at the expense of locals. Windsor and Eton had no workmen's trains.

The interest in the situation, in regard to aliens moving to other places, was so great that *The Times* actually published a story in April about someone trying to falsely use a ticket on the railway that was not theirs. Not the type of story one would expect to find in *The Times*, but of course the person involved was an alien, which made the story more newsworthy. A lady from Maidenhead, Mrs Dora Schwartz, had three seasons' tickets for travel between Aldgate and Maidenhead. These were for Mr Schwartz, Master Israel Schwartz, and Miss Bloomer Schwartz. On the date in question Mrs Schwartz and two other women tried to use the season tickets at Aldgate, but were stopped by the ticket inspector. Mr and Mrs Schwartz were fined £2 each and made to pay costs. The tickets were then confiscated.

The success of the German advance on the Western Front in March saw a new outbreak of hatred against the aliens who had not yet been interned. Even some street names that sounded German were changed. The German success also led to more men being removed from industry to the Army. This new plan to raise more men also included conscription for the Irish, but this idea was later dropped.

April saw the expansion of rationing with meat, butter, and margarine added to sugar. The population were provided with ration cards. This was a difficult situation in itself and in Colchester schools were closed for a week while teachers were used to write out the ration cards for the population of the town. The amount of food available weekly was not large, but at least everyone was guaranteed their supply. Some local councils, especially in poorer areas, opened more national kitchens where food could be bought to take home, which were on the ration card.

It was not only aliens from the east end who were moving to Reading. At the end of April a police constable was suspicious of three men in Burghfield near the town. He said goodnight to the men who did not reply. Knowing that there were escaped prisoners at large he grabbed one of the men. There was a scuffle and Constable Jordan, who had been invalided out of the Household Cavalry due to a wound, was overpowered; one of the men had a knife. The men ran off into the woods, but the next day there was a search of the woods and Constable Jordan and some special constables recaptured the men who had escaped from Bramley Internment Camp. This is one of the few cases I have found where violence was used by escapees when attempts were made to apprehend them. It was more usual that escaped prisoners gave themselves up as soon as they were discovered.

Although there were a number of prisoners from both sides were interned in Holland, the supply of food for them and the Dutch population was becoming a problem. In April the Allies offered to supply the country with cereals. The Dutch, however, wanted guarantees that any ships that they sent to collect the cereals would not be requisitioned. It was thought that Germany could not reasonably object to Dutch ships leaving Holland if they were sure to return. At the same time Germany was trying to arrange the supply of goods to Belgium through Holland. It seemed that every attempt at agreements between the warring factions led to requests for favours in return, which often seemed to benefit the Germans. In April there was deadlock in the attempted agreement at the exchange of prisoners. The German government would not agree unless the British Government would guarantee that the German civilians in China were neither interned nor deported. If this was agreed then the Germans were prepared to continue with negotiations on exchanges and would endeavour to exempt the labour of all British prisoners in salt mines and restrict their use in coal mines. The British government could not give such a guarantee as it was based on the decision of the Chinese government. The German offer was to agree a man-for-man exchange of combatants, excluding officers held for eighteen months, in exchange for German civilians throughout the British Empire who wished to leave. They would give one British civilian, including merchant seamen and one combatant for every four German civilians. The combatants would be from those interned in Holland and Switzerland. All British and German officers in Holland would be repatriated and all 1,600 German civilians in Holland would be exchanged for the 400 British.

In Germany, Rudolf Rocker had still been held in the school waiting for a decision on his future to arrive from Berlin. It eventually came in April when it was decided that as he had been out of the country for more than ten years he had lost his German citizenship and would not be allowed back in. This was the result he had hoped for and he was to be sent back to Holland. When he arrived in Holland they were suspicious—they had never heard of anyone being stripped of their nationality. He was told that anyone without means would be interned, but he asked if he could go and live with a friend and this was agreed.

There were two German seaman captured somewhere on the south coast in May just as they were about to steal a boat and attempt to cross the channel. They were part of a group of four who had escaped from Lark Hill camp. They said that they did not know the whereabouts of the other two men who had escaped with them. Two other men who had escaped from King's Lynn camp were also recaptured in May.

There was an interesting report on crime in the Isle of Man for the previous year published in *The Times* in May. Enemy aliens had been responsible for the majority of the crimes committed on the island. Ninety-one internees were committed to prison on the island in 1917, while only forty-five locals were. This may have been due to the crime of escaping, which the locals did not do, but the aliens did.

There had supposedly been constant refusals by the government to take any form of reprisal against German prisoners in retaliation to the bad treatment of British prisoners in Germany throughout the war. Then, in May, Lord Newton announced that there would be reprisals as a result of continued German mistreatment of British prisoners. This was due to the failure by all other means to get the Germans to improve conditions. I believe that there had been reprisals in a number of cases, although these were usually hidden behind other reasons for the treatment of German prisoners. The main concern at the time was of the treatment of prisoners by the commander of the 10 Army Corps under whose command the conditions of British officers had been intolerable. Despite the claims of retaliation being taken against German officers in one of the camps, Newton did not explain what these measures would involve.

There were new takers of German prisoners towards the end of April as the American troops began to take a part in the fighting. At Cantigny the Germans were reported to be angry at being taken prisoner by Americans. The prisoners were described as dull-looking men in dirty grey uniforms, looking like slugs or earthworms

There were rail travel restrictions imposed in Britain in May, but they seem to have been rather haphazard. If they were an attempt to stop the evacuation of those from London to the towns along the Thames then they were not very effective. The price of fares was raised and there was some restriction on the sale of season tickets, but those who had bought season tickets since January could still buy them, which would include many of those who had already moved out of London since then.

The end of May saw the arrest in Ireland of members of Sinn Féin after further rumours of a German-Irish plot of involvement in a German invasion. The government claimed to have evidence, though refused to reveal what it was. There had been stories of the inmates of Oldcastle Internment Camp joining such a plot in the past and 450 of the inhabitants of the camp were deported. They arrived in Dublin by train and boarded a special steamer. The men arrested included a number of well-known figures such as Edward de Valera (a member of parliament who had refused to take his seat) and George Noble Plunkett (a member of parliament). There had supposedly been plans for another uprising aided by German troops in 1917, which was delayed due to America entering the war. There had been another uprising planned for 1918 and a man had been captured landing from a German submarine in April and was being held in the Tower of London.

May saw the beginning of the exchange of large numbers of German and French prisoners. There had been an agreement signed at Berne in April between the two powers. Italy had also agreed a similar plan that had come as a surprise to the British. Lord Newton said in the commons at the end of May that Britain had entered talks with the Germans to try and arrange a similar plan. The Franco-German plan was for all prisoners held for more than eighteen months in France and Germany who would be exchanged man-for-man and rank-for-rank. Many of those interned in Switzerland would also be released. The total numbers involved were thought to be around 150,000 on both sides, but due to transport problems only around 10,000 a month would be released. As the year progressed, there were more prisoners being released from some camps. One of these had been interned in Austria, which seemed to have escaped much criticism until now. The man was not named, but was quoted in an article in the *New York Times Current History Magazine*. He described how internees in the country were held at either camps or stations where internees were charged more to live. He described a camp at Illmau where internees were kept in a dark cellar and told by the guard that they would die there. Inspectors were shown only the above ground part of the camp and told no one was in the cellars. Punishment was often carried out by stringing up—the hands were tied behind the back and then pulled up by a rope and kept there until the victim fainted. Drossendorf was another camp where the internees were treated badly. At this camp women were kept in the same room as men with very basic sanitary facilities. There were a number of Russians in this camp and some died of starvation. Other camps at Katzanau and Estergom in Hungary were said to be just as bad.

A quartermaster, Sergeant T. Duggan of the Coldstream Guards, was held in a camp at Schneidemühl, Germany, from 1914 to March 1918. There were British Belgians and Russians in the camp. At first there were no quarters available and the prisoners lived in holes in the ground and in December, 1914, there was a typhus epidemic. There were 40,000 prisoners at the camp and there were an average of thirty deaths a day.

There was a meeting of representatives of metropolitan councils in Westminster City Hall in early July when the topic of enemy aliens was discussed. It was said that there were 30,000 aliens interned, but that 13,000 were still at large. This was due to reasons such as long residence in the country, being married to English wives, or having sons in the British forces. Mr H. J. Ormond, mayor of Stoke Newington, said that 'it was due to being seen as harsh treatment to intern these people that had escaped internment, but this was to weigh against the hardship inflicted on our own people'. Ormond went on to argue that in many cases the reasons for these aliens being free was based on flimsy evidence of their not being a danger. He did not give any explanation of how their continued freedom was having any influence on the hardship on our own people. He then called on the government to intern every alien over eighteen years of age; a view that was agreed with by the majority of the other persons present.

During July the German government agreed in principle to send grain from Germany to Holland for the German prisoners held there. There had also been recent arrivals in the country of British prisoners from Germany. These included officers, non-commissioned officers, and a number of merchant seamen.

A Mr David Davis, justice of the peace and alderman of West Ham, appeared at West Ham Police court in July. He was charged with failing to keep a register of alien lodgers at a lodging house that he owned at Victoria Dock Road. A German named Martin had escaped from an internment camp and had been working at the docks. He had been discovered and sentenced to six months hard labour. He had been staying at the lodging house for ten weeks, but there was no record of it in the register. It was said in court that Davis devoted a great deal of his time to public work. He did not live at the house and had told his employee Mr Horne that no aliens were to be admitted to the house. Martin had not only deceived Mr Horne, but also the people at the dock where he worked. The charges were dismissed.

There was to be a Commons debate on the alien question in July and six members of the house were asked by the Prime Minister to make a thorough investigation of the various phases of the enemy alien question. One of the members of the group was Mr Joynson-Hicks, a man who had been calling for stricter enforcement of aliens for some time. The rest of the group were also men who had been of a similar view. The actions were it seems due to the constant calls for a review of the continued freedom of many aliens.

It was no surprise when the group reported back with the view that there should be more internment and that all alien-run businesses should be closed down. There were some views given that it was believed that there were different rules for rich and poor aliens in that those who were well off with important contacts were often given exemption. Perhaps one of the suggestions in the report that did make sense was that there were eight different departments dealing with the law on enemy aliens and that this should be unified. The group's report resulted in a new aliens' policy that led to the review of the circumstances of all those exempted from internment. There was a review of naturalisation certificates and no employment of aliens was allowed in government offices unless they were the child of natural born subjects of this country or that of an Allied country. Exceptions were allowed in this rule where there was a definite national reason. Identity books were to be issued to all aliens and the powers given to close alien businesses. A committee was set up to review the cases of enemy aliens who had been previously exempt from internment. They were authorised to appoint any person to hold an inquiry that they considered necessary.

The negotiations over the exchange of prisoners had been going on for some time and in July, only months before the war was to end, an agreement was reached. The Germans had agreed to move officers from the camps at Holzminden and Clausthal to other officer camps.

This was in return for the British moving German officers from Dyffren Aled to other officer's camps after complaints about that camp and Kegworth. The German camps were to be evacuated and improvements made at the British camps. The agreement went on to state that officers who had been prisoners for more than eighteen months would be exchanged head-for-head. All prisoners held in Holland and Switzerland would be released. The crews of submarines held for more than eighteen months would be interned in Holland. The agreement reinforced points that had been in force since the beginning of the war, but may have been ignored in many cases. Prisoners of war were to be protected from violence and public curiosity, and they were not to be compelled to do any work connected with the operations of the war. It was also not allowed to compel them forcibly to give details about their army or their country. The transport of the German prisoners in Britain's overseas dominions was to be on four German passenger steamers under the command of Dutch naval officers. The British prisoners in Holland and Switzerland would be taken by ship to Britain. The agreement between the British and Germans was to be overseen by the Dutch. However, the Dutch government stipulated that due to the increasing difficulties of their financial position it was happy to offer hospitality to prisoners of war depending on the settlement of questions relating to an economic nature.

Although small fines were often given for fraternisation, there were occasions when stricter punishments were given for those consorting with prisoners. At Marks Cross petty sessions the wife of the licensee of a hotel in Wadhurst was sentenced to three months hard labour for fraternisation. Elizabeth Gibbs had been charged with sending uncensored letters and cigarettes to a German prisoner of war. The letters were described as impassioned and abandoned and were sent without the knowledge of Gibb's husband. The woman had encouraged a corporal of the guard at the camp to pass on the letters by paying him 10s to deliver them. She told the prisoner that she was the daughter of the licensee of the hotel, not his wife, and looked forward to the time when she and the prisoner could be married. Perhaps the woman's mental state would have been taken into consideration at a later time.

There were a number of offences in relation to prisoners that led to court appearances. At Tottenham, Walter Fuller, a member of the Royal Defence Corps, was charged with being an absentee. He was one of two men responsible for guarding German prisoners who were working on a farm in Essex. The two men took it in turns to guard the prisoners while the other went about his own business, which meant that they only had one guard at a time.

By August 1918 there were over 700 German prisoners working on farms in Cheshire. Men travelled from Handforth Camp to farms within a 3-mile radius, leaving in groups of up to ten prisoners on a farm with a single unarmed guard, who dropped them off at several farms. The guard only stayed if there were more than three men at one farm. Guards picked the men up again in the evening, or if they were working late the farmer himself dropped them off at the camp. There were twenty-six unarmed guards who took 200 men to eighty-six farms. The system was different elsewhere in the country. In Devon a number of small camps were set up, each holding around fifty prisoners; these men then went out each day in small groups to work on farms near to their camps. The farmers were responsible for the prisoners and in some cases the prisoners were even allowed to live on the farm, being fed by the farmer rather than by those at the camp. The scheme was not entirely without problems. In Berkshire four prisoners carrying out farm work were arrested for assaulting a girl of sixteen. Fraternisation by women with prisoners also took place, and that was seen as a problem by the authorities. In Aldershot, for example, two members of the Women's Royal Air Force were brought up before the local magistrates, charged under regulation 46a, which prohibited helping prisoners to escape or giving those articles likely to help them escape. The girls had received a letter from the prisoners at Cove Camp thanking them for cigarettes. It seems there were several cases of women approaching prisoners and giving presents or sending letters to them. There were calls for more severe penalties for women who persisted in illegal communication with prisoners.

Although the success of prisoners working in Cheshire had been praised in the press in August, there was some problems with German POW workers there in September when they went on strike. The men had been working on drainage between Frodsham and *The* Manchester ship canal when some were taken off to help with harvesting. Those left on drainage work went on strike because those on harvest were paid more than them and harvesting was better work. The strikers were put on bread and water rations and their mail was withheld. The strike ended after two days. *The Manchester Guardian* said that the strike by POWs was unusual in that it was for higher wages. There had been strikes by British POWs in Germany, but these were usually about living conditions. There were at the time now 800 Germans employed on the land in Cheshire. Two new depots had been set up at Hatherton and Cuddington each with forty men. It was not only German prisoners who were helping out on the land. The *War Illustrated* published a number of photographs of various groups helping out on farms, including Girl Guides and Boy Scouts at Leigh on Sea, schoolboys from Leicester County Council Schools were digging the city parks for planting food, and even British soldiers were working on some farms, which would seem a misuse of men who surely could have been doing more worthwhile work in France.

A deputation from the National Union of Women Workers approached the Home Secretary in September. They were campaigning for the right of British women who were married to aliens being able to retain their British citizenship. This had been the case until 1870. A committee was set up to look into the matter. There was also some dispute over whether all aliens with sons serving in the British forces were exempt from interment. The Alien's Advisory Committee said that this was not always the case as there was evidence that some aliens had tried to deter their children from joining the forces or even punished them for doing so and in these cases internment was used. The fact that a son was in the British Army did not in any way determine the loyalty of his father.

The most serious cases of spying led to the suspects being held in the Tower of London where some of them were executed, while others were held in internment camps. *The Manchester Guardian* described Burd Johannen Bon Grueber as a most dangerous spy when he escaped from a Yorkshire internment camp in September. The report did not clarify whether it was a military or civilian camp he had escaped from, and the report said he may be wearing a field grey uniform or civilian clothing.

October saw the return of a number of British prisoners from Germany along with some of those who had been interned in Holland. They arrived at Hull and were welcomed by large crowds. There were some who had escaped captivity in Germany altogether and spent the rest of the war in Holland. The prisoners were welcomed with a speech written by the king and read out by Sir Stanley Donop. There seemed to have been some evidence that the treatment of British prisoners in the hands of the Germans had improved as the war had gone on. In October, however, there was a report by the Younger Committee on the ill treatment of British captives. The report was based on evidence given by men taken prisoner during the spring offensive by the Germans and who had since escaped. The report admitted that the number of prisoners taken by the Germans during the offensive had no doubt exceeded the amounts they had expected and this had overwhelmed their expectations. This may have explained why in many cases the prisoners were not fed for up to forty-eight hours and did not have adequate accommodation. Some of the German officers told the prisoners that the lack of food was due to the British blockade, while others said that it was in reprisal for how German prisoners were being treated in Britain; this was despite a statement by a German general at Villiers in April, stating that they knew that their men were being well treated in Britain. The committee were told of another German officer who told the prisoners that they would break their brave English hearts. Some of the men said that the Germans always seemed to have plenty of food, despite using shortages as a reason for starving them. They were also often kept in the open with no shelter at all and were forced to march all day and stop in the open by the side of the road at night. Many of the prisoners were set to work and, aside from a drink at 4 a.m., they had nothing to drink or eat until 7 p.m. The guards would strike anyone who stopped work with the butts of their rifles and the rule was that anyone trying to escape would be shot with no warning. Many of the prisoners were forced to carry shells close to the front where they were under fire by their own large guns and four prisoners were killed by shells at Villiers. There were also claims that prisoners were killed after surrendering. On 21 March at Lagnicourt some men were defending a trench and were surrounded, the Germans beckoned the men to come forward and the first three to leave the trench were shot as they climbed out. On the same day at Bullecourt five men were captured. As the first man climbed out of a trench a German private ran at him with his bayonet fixed; he refused to stop at an order from a German officer who then shot the man in the head.

It was not only in Germany that British prisoners were mistreated; those taken by the Turks were at even more of a disadvantage. Of a total of 16,583 prisoners taken 3,290 had been reported dead and 2,222 remained untraced, believed to be dead. All the untraced belonged to the garrison at Kut. They died in a march they were forced to undertake across the Syrian Desert. It seems strange that the numerous reports of bad treatment by the Germans in relation to British prisoners that appeared in the press that there was hardly a mention of any problems with those held by the Turks. A memorial tablet in a church in Tilbury, Essex, to a soldier, 'taken by the Turk and never seen again,' says it all.

There had been previous incidences when German prisoner workers had gone on strike, but this was normally to do with food or money. In October an unusual reason for them to stop work was given. The event occurred in a camp in the south of England where the prisoners were making roads. The prison workers were sent a number of conscientious objectors to help with the task and refused to carry on working. The German non-commissioned officer with the workers explained to the British officer in charge that they would not work with men who refused to fight for their country. He told the officer that they would accept any punishment they were given rather than work with the men. The conscientious objectors were withdrawn and the Germans carried on with their work.

The end of October saw a statement by the Home Secretary published in *The Manchester Guardian*. He had claimed in the Commons that if the war ended either by peace or armistice a primary condition would be the immediate release of all our prisoners of war in enemy countries—his view may have been a little optimistic.

Although the camp at Ruhleben was known to be harsh on internees at the beginning of its use, things quickly began to change and (according to Percy Brown who was one of the inmates) things were not too bad. While others went short of food, those in the camp did not. They received plenty of parcels from home as well as bread from bakeries that the British government had set up in Holland. Brown said that they often read in smuggled British newspapers how they were suffering in the camp. There was a separate barracks for black men who were interned in the camp. These men came from a variety of countries and many did not know why they were interned. This seemed to reflect the situation for many of those interned in Britain. Many of them did not care who won the war and just wanted it to end so they could go home. There was also an answer to those still calling for retaliation against German prisoners in Britain from the Home Secretary. He said that it would be simpler and more merciful to just shoot them than to torture, insult, and degrade them as our men had been in certain camps. The war was almost over and it was not the time to penalise German prisoners. According to the Home Secretary no complaint of mistreatment could be directed towards Austria-Hungary, but that Turkey had rivalled Germany in her cruelties. He said that no more than half the prisoners taken at Kut would return alive. The situation of the British prisoners in Germany was unclear as the war ended. At a camp in Schweidnitz, J. B. Sterndal Benet described how the guards were ripping imperial eagles from their uniforms. The prisoners were told that the Kaiser had fled, but that their situation was still not clear. They were told that they could leave the camp if they wanted, but that they could be in danger from the local population. The prisoners were then visited by a representative from a Soldiers and Workers Council. It was such organisations that were in control of many areas in Germany just after the war ended. The man told them that machine guns were being installed at the camp for the protection of the prisoners. This seemed strange when the guns were aimed at the prisoners rather than in the direction from which any threat would have come from the outside. The prisoners were eventually allowed out of the camp and could visit the town. It was evident to them that the German population could not understand why the departure of the Kaiser had not ended all the problems and shortages that they had suffered through the war. Red Cross supplies increased for the prisoners and they often fed treats to the German children in the town.

It was to be four weeks after the armistice before the prisoners were able to leave the town and the locals cheered them as they departed. They took a train to Danzig where they were loaded aboard a ship for home and landed at Leith on Christmas Day. They were welcomed by the Gordon Highlanders Band and given breakfast in in the sheds at the quayside.

By the end of November there had been some relaxation of the restrictions on the British wives or the widows of aliens, although there were exemptions in certain cases. The majority now only had to notify the police of a change of address, carry identity cards, and to register at hotels.

As well as the hardships, which were a result of the war, the British population also had to contend with the Spanish Flu epidemic that had grown worse as the year went on and in many cases proved to be fatal. In some parts of the country the Army had to be brought in to help with the dead and there were often queues of funerals outside churches.

Although the war was over the German prisoners in Britain were to continue to be held until the Peace Treaty was ratified. In France many of the prisoners held by the Americans were being forced to clear old ordnance, which turned out to be very dangerous and did lead to some deaths.

6

1919

While some of the interned had been released as early as February 1917 many of the internees at Ruhleben, Berlin, were not finally released until 1919 by the Revolutionary Government. Those being released told how conditions in the camp for the first year of the war had been terrible, although conditions improved in late 1915 mainly due to the food being sent from home. Of those released early they were mainly those who were interned late in the war, one of those released was reported in *The Times*; Gustave Hille had not been interned until August 1918 and had only spent a few months in a camp. The reason for releasing some internees early was that they had British wives and children, some of whom were serving in the British forces. Their early release was perhaps an admission that they should not have been interned at all and the fact that they had been interned so late showed that for much of the war they had not been seen as dangerous. Another group of men who had been imprisoned during the war were the conscientious objectors. They were not all freed as soon as the war ended either. In March 1919 there were still over 1,000 of them in prison and over 3,000 in camps carrying out labour service—as an added punishment they were not allowed to vote for five years after the war.

At the outbreak of war, the idea of passports were seen as unneeded by the majority of people. This changed during the conflict and by the end of January there was a great demand for the documents, even amongst British citizens. There had been no decision by the government as to whether the passport would be retained, but as there were plans to stop Germans entering the country their retention seemed likely. It was not only foreigners who needed passports, many British citizens wanting to visit places such as America were applying for them. The passport office was not used to such demand and *The Times* published a complaint from a British gentleman who had queued outside the office, in the rain, with 600 other people. Queueing was the norm in the last years of the war so one would have thought that the population would have been used to it. The need for a passport to visit America was due to government discussions in Washington as to how they would restrict the entry of aliens into the country for four years after the end of the war. There were exceptions to the ban, which included government officials and a number of professions such as teachers, religious ministers, and doctors.

There is always criticism of actions taken by the government during a war when what they introduce has no effect and the Martello Towers during the Napoleonic Wars were a good example. Perhaps their critics may have preferred invasion by the French so that they could have been used and their erection justified. There was similar criticism of the National Shipyards in *The Times* in March. The three National Shipyards had been opened at Chepstow, Beachley, and Portbury on the rivers Wye and Severn. The plan was that they would produce the ships to replace those sunk by German U-boats; there were 6,000 workers moved there from other shipbuilding areas and 200 houses were built for them. German prisoners were also moved there to help with the work, the whole population of a nearby village had been evicted with only days' notice to make room for their camp. The issue caused was that only one ship was built in the three yards. Perhaps the critics would have preferred the war to have gone on longer so the yards could have been seen as being of more value for money. According to *The Times* the whole scheme had been a 'crying scandal'. It does seem as though the work at the site was poorly organised, but if the war had gone on the yard may well have proved its worth. The German prisoners at the yards were described as well fed and cheerful, possessing plenty of tobacco and cigarettes, which measured just how well they were treated. They were moving about in batches, apparently marking time and there were many other workers still employed in the yards, despite there being no work going on. The report also stated that the large hospital built on the site for workers had never been used. It was claimed that the local VAD hospital in Chepstow was asked if they could move their patients to the hospital while a government inspector was visiting so that it looked like it was being used. Perhaps the complaints did then have some basis.

In March the Archbishop of Canterbury asked about the interned aliens and what was going to happen to them. He said that during the war it had been necessary to intern aliens, but he believed that it would eventually be revealed that very few of these people had in fact been of any danger or even under suspicion of any acts of sabotage. What was going to happen now that the fighting was over; at the time of the armistice there were still 22,000 civilians in British camps. Of these 10,000 had now been repatriated, but 12,000 still remained. It was said that these people had been offered the choice of repatriation or of remaining in camps, although there had been promises by the government that all enemy aliens would be repatriated. The Government reply from the Earl of Jersey was that all internees who had wanted to go were repatriated and those that remained wanted to stay in Britain. At the present time the government had made no decision as to what the rules for allowing enemy aliens to stay were and no answer to this could be expected in the near future. There would be new tribunals who would hear the cases of those wanting to stay and they would then make a decision.

The release of Germans from internment was not the only problem for the government when it came to releasing men. There had been several cases of unrest amongst British and colonial troops who had expected to be demobilised straight after the war. There had even been cases of troops rioting when they were refused release from the Army. Many of the members of the Army were shocked to find that they were going to be part of the British occupation forces in Germany instead of going home. In March the situation for a number of returned British prisoners of war came to a head at Fort Gomer, near Gosport. The 300 men who had been prisoners of war in Germany were ordered to guard German prisoner of war camps. They objected to the duty and marched to Portsmouth where they sought an interview with the mayor. They believed that as ex-prisoners of war they should be entitled to preferential consideration in demobilisation, after what they had suffered at the hands of the Germans they did not think that they should have to guard German prisoners. The mayor convinced them to return to camp and promised to speak to the authorities about their complaint.

By March there were still more than 60,000 German military prisoners working for wages of between a halfpenny and a tuppence an hour. This was mainly in agriculture and road building or drainage.

They were almost all employed in England and Wales, there were very few in Scotland. Those no longer needed for work were being sent to France when transport became available.

April saw the introduction of a new Aliens Bill. It was essentially the same bill introduced in 1914, but was now to be in force in peacetime as well as during the war. Although the bill did not differentiate between friendly and enemy aliens the Home Office would have that power. The bill would prohibit aliens landing in the country and impose conditions on any that did. It would prohibit them from living in certain areas and to register any change of address. It would also impose penalties on those who aid or abet any breaking of the order. The new bill was severely criticised in the Commons at its second reading. Most of the critics felt that the bill did not go far enough in banning aliens from the country. One of its critics was Horatio Bottomly, MP for Hackney South and also the editor of *John Bull* magazine. His criticism of the lenient treatment of aliens during the war was to continue in peacetime. He claimed that the country had for too long been the dumping ground of refugees and wanted all aliens banned from entering the country. Mr Bottomley was later imprisoned for a fraud concerning war bonds. Perhaps there was something in what Bottomley had to say. If there had not been so many aliens in Britain at the outbreak of war then there would not have been so many problems due to internment. Another criticism was that the bill would allow floods of foreign workers to enter the country at the expense of British workers. Labour members of Parliament were criticised for not speaking out against the danger of the alien population towards the British working classes. Many of the politicians who had been campaigning for sterner action over enemy aliens were still at it and in July the standing committee on the alien's restriction bill voted in favour of making it a statutory obligation to deport all enemy aliens except those with specific grounds for exemption. The clause was introduced by Sir John Butcher, Bottomley, and Joynson-Hicks among others. They wanted all aliens deported within one month of the passing of the act. The government were opposed to this, despite Sir John Butchers claim that there had been 21,000 enemy aliens at liberty in November the previous year and 5,000 Germans in April. The response by the government was to claim that many enemy aliens had been repatriated and those with exemptions were having their cases reconsidered by Mr Justice Sankey's committee. There was still a tendency of those calling for strict action in regard to aliens to group all foreigners together as enemies. This was shown when Sir Herbert Nield claimed that there was still a dangerous German element in the east end of London. Sir William Pearce then stated that the east end alien population consisted almost entirely of Russian and Polish Jews not Germans.

While some in this country were calling for Germans to be sent home the German Government were asking for the same thing. There was some disagreement over those prisoners who had been found guilty of an offence in this country while in captivity. The most extreme example of this was a German soldier who had broken into the house of a farmer on whose farm he had been working and had murdered the farmer and his wife. The man's death sentence had been postponed until peace was signed. Justice would not have been served if this offender was reprieved. In June a telegram from the German government stated that since the conclusion of the Armistice, German prisoners in the hands of the Allies had been totally cut off from communication with their homes. They went on to ask that the prisoners in Britain be given higher pay, better accommodation, and more freedom of movement. Because the peace treaty still had to be ratified POWs were not released straight away. In July 1919 there were still thousands of German prisoners held in Britain, although the sick and wounded had been sent home. The French wanted to borrow many of the British prisoners as labour, but this was refused. Many were still working in agriculture and in filling trenches, which was causing some conflict with British workers coming home from the Army. There had been a request from the French Government that German prisoners in Britain should be sent to France where they would be used as workers. The British government had refused, but then it was pointed out at a meeting of the Supreme Council that the prisoners held by the British in France and Belgium were a great expense. It was suggested that the French should take over these prisoners for use as labour instead of those held in Britain.

Ratification of the peace treaty was anticipated at a meeting in Paris in August 1919, and repatriation of military prisoners began soon afterwards. This was dependent on a commission due to meet in Paris, which would discuss the German prisoners. Germany was expected to pay for their repatriation. The committee meeting in Paris to discuss the repatriation of German prisoners decided at the end of August that they would, in anticipation of the ratification of the peace treaty, begin the repatriation immediately. This would take place under an inter-Allied committee to which a German interest would be added once the treaty was signed.

It was no surprise that some of the German military prisoners may have been unhappy at their continued captivity despite the war being over. The attempts at escape therefore went on and in August there were a number of escapes. There were four from Whitehaven, two from Southminster, two from Lofthouse Park, and one from Wakefield. Four escapees from Bulford had also been recaptured.

There were problems with some of the German prisoners working on farms, many of them claimed that they could not work a full day because they were not given enough to eat. This resulted in one farmer, Rupert Brown of Barkingside, appearing at Stratford Police Court in east London at the end of August. Brown employed a number of Germans at his Gaysham Hall Farm. They did heavy work from 7 a.m. to 5 p.m. and he noticed that they did not do a full day's work for the 7*d* an hour he paid them. They claimed that they could not work so long on the 8 oz of dry bread and tea that they were given. The commandant of the camp the men came from told Brown that they could have no more food. Brown claimed that in the best interests of the country he sold the men more bread so that they could work harder. His actions were he said in no way in sympathy with the men. Whatever his reasons were he was fined £20. Another local farmer James Torrance of New Barns farm, Chigwell, also gave his German workers more food. He was only fined £10, as unlike Brown he had not charged them for the food. Providing Germans with food was obviously still a serious offence. There were a number of German prisoners filling in a trench near Whitley in August. They were under the guard of a private England when they were approached by a man who asked if he could give the prisoners some bananas. England replied that no one was allowed to give prisoners anything and the man replied that he would risk it and left. Shortly after this the man returned in a motor car with a box of apples, which he began to throw to the Germans. The prisoners then rushed over and gathered around the man's car. Sergeant Prince who was in command of the work party said that it took about half an hour to get the men back to work. The man was charged and appeared in Whitley Bay Court; he was a doctor named Horseman and he told the court that peace was signed and that we were no longer at war with Germany. Horseman hoped that in future all nations would be at peace with each other and let bygones be bygones. The court obviously did not agree and fined him £25.

When the armistice had been signed there were 750,000 prisoners in the hands of the Allies, the majority of these were in France. There had already been more than 7,000 repatriated from Britain and of the 96,000 still in the country more than 40,000 were employed, nearly 10,000 were in hospital or unfit, 21,000 were officers or senior NCO's, 3,500 employed in camp duties, 10,000 awaiting transport to France, and 11,500 were unemployed.

A number of internment camps had already been closed such as the ones at Ripon, Spalding, Douglas, and Hackney due to the 23,073 civil prisoners who had already been repatriated. Alexandria Palace was also being emptied, but there were more than 3,000 civil prisoners still held whose cases were being considered for exemption from repatriation. A number of German prisoners had been returned to Germany by September and large numbers of them were handed over in Cologne, which was part of the British occupation of Germany. It was thought that the British would provide transport and that they would hand over 3,000 prisoners a day at Cologne. They would also send prisoners to Rotterdam in British ships. The return of German prisoners in France would have seemed to have been easier than the movement of those from Britain, but they were being held until the ratification of the peace treaty. The French were not as eager to return their prisoners. The repatriation of the prisoners from Britain was almost completed by October, though the return of the Germans was not popular everywhere; trains carrying the prisoners were stoned as they travelled through Belgium—after this the trains ran at night. The German prisoners held by the French were facing different problems. The French were still not ready to send all the prisoners home. They told the German government that they had anticipated the ratification of the Peace Treaty, but that the return of prisoners was dependent on the fulfilment by the Germans of their obligations. The Germans claimed that these obligations were deliveries of coal and paying the fine in the Mannerheim Case, which would then result in the return of those prisoners held in France once those held in Britain had been returned.

Not all the prisoners held in Britain had been repatriated by November. There were still 1,600 prisoners in Park Hall Camp at Oswestry. They had been working on clearing up, but refused to work as they had grown unhappy with the fact that most of the other prisoners had been sent home. They went on strike, but finally returned to work when their rations were stopped.

By November many of the decisions on the exemption of civil prisoners had been made and according to *The Times* 16 per cent of those interned at the signing of the armistice had been allowed to stay by the Alien's Repatriation Committee, led by Lord Justice Younger. The committee had considered more than 4,000 cases, many of these were old men who had lived in the country for some time. There were also a number of men of military age who had British wives and young children who spoke no German and knew no other country than ours. Others had children who had served in the British forces during the war. In all cases they had refused the chance of immediate freedom and repatriation to their country of origin to remain in the camps until a decision was reached on their fate. Of those given exemption from repatriation there were 3,030 Germans, 840 Austrians, and twenty Turks. Of the Germans, 2,230 had British born wives or children and there were 400 who had lived in Britain for more than thirty years or since they were less than fifteen years old when they arrived.

The presence of aliens was still causing some problems into 1920, when in January the government decided to carry on paying allowances to destitute aliens. This included the dependants of Russians and the British born wives of those aliens who had been deported, but whose wives had stayed.

There were still cases being heard against those who disagreed with their status and in January the Court of Appeal heard the case of Heinrich Markwald. Markwald had been born in Germany, but in 1908 had obtained a certificate of British naturalisation in Australia. He came to Britain shortly after this and in 1914 was told to register as an alien, which he refused to do. He was prosecuted, but had appealed—the appeal was dismissed.

Despite the report in the previous November that just over 4,000 enemy aliens had been given permission to stay in the country it was reported in *The Times* in February that there were still more than 13,000 Germans still in the country. There were also 8,278 Austrians and 333 Turks.

In April the Alien's Order came into force, which stated that foreign residents were still required to register with the police. Foreign visitors who had permission from the immigration officer were allowed to stay two months instead of one before they had to register. After this they must report all movements to the police or provide the name of a British subject who would be responsible for revealing their whereabouts at any time.

There were attempts to bring to justice those who had been guilty of war crimes in Germany. There were 900 suspects and in May trials were held in Leipzig. There were nine men charged with war crimes, involving the mistreatment of POWs and with crimes at sea. Those found guilty received short prison sentences; this was not well accepted in Britain where it was thought that the sentences were too lenient—in Germany they were seen as too severe.

By the end of 1920 there were new worries about aliens and in October a man appeared in court at Bow Street who had failed to register and refused to answer questions put to him. He was suspected of being a courier between a revolutionary party in Britain and the Soviet Government. The man had been seen by special branch officers in the company of a woman who was a member of the British Communist Party.

The man had in his possession when arrested an attaché case containing a number of letters, one was from Sylvia Pankhurst, who was at that time under remand on a charge of sedition, addressed to Lenin. There was another one from Pankhurst to Zinovieff, a well-known member of the revolutionary government, and a letter in cipher, which had not been decoded. It seemed that the war was over, but there was a new enemy to worry about.

Conclusion

There seems to be little dispute of the fact that German prisoners in Britain were treated much better than the majority of the British prisoners who were held in Germany. Inspections of British camps found content and well-fed men who they were allowed to speak to and who were able to make complaints. Inspectors could turn up at any time at camps in Britain and be admitted. Those who inspected German camps normally had to announce the planned visit beforehand, which often allowed the camp guards to prepare for the visit and make changes to the normal routine. For example, one man at Sennelager Camp claimed that he lived in tents full of holes and they were given new tents for an inspection and moved back to the old tents once it was finished; inspectors were often not allowed to speak to prisoners without an officer being present. Perhaps the greatest proof of the difference in treatment of POWs was in the condition of exchanged prisoners. The Dutch press commented on how the German prisoners returning from Britain were well fed and well clothed, while those returning from Germany were often physical wrecks, garbed in tattered thin and odd clothing with every sign of bad feeding and ill treatment.

There is no doubt that many of the reports of the time by both British and German sources were highly influenced by propaganda. There was an interesting quote by Paul Cohen-Portheim in relation to this who said that during the war 'truth was dead and that propaganda had replaced it'. It is widely believed that the British won the propaganda war, they had managed to convince much of the world that the Germans were a race of people who would let nothing stand in their way of victory; this included civilians and even neutrals. There was an interesting argument in Morgan's book on German atrocities. Morgan claimed that throughout history wars had been increasingly improving the situation of non-combatants and that wars would only be fought between regular disciplined forces on both sides. He stated that this was not the case in the First World War, non-combatants had been slaughtered in Belgium and Northern France by the Germans. He also went on to include the death of civilians on the ships that were sunk by German U-boats. Interestingly he did not mention the deaths of civilians in air raids. Perhaps due to the fact that the Allies were carrying out just as many raids of their own and in fact more later on in the war. Military targets may have been the main aim, but there is little doubt that German civilians died during these raids just as British and French civilians did at the hands of German bombers. However, there does seem to be enough reports, by those without a vested interest, to confirm that the British treated their military captives in a much more civilised way than the majority of those in German captivity. Although, this does not deny the fact that (in some cases) the men in command of German camps did do their best to treat their prisoners fairly in what were quite difficult circumstances. I believe much of the harsh treatment was due to the way that German officers were used to treating their own men, which was reflected in the treatment of prisoners.

The greatest opportunity for atrocities to be committed against prisoners was between the time of their capture and their being delivered to a camp. There are a number of claims of serious violence towards Allied prisoners by the German troops who captured them, but I am certain that they were examples of atrocities against German prisoners as well. I am also sure that not all the stories about atrocities were true.

Robert Graves claimed that every officer in the mess could quote specific examples of German prisoners being mistreated by Allied troops. In his opinion this often happened in revenge for the death of friends or family at enemy hands or even because the men who took prisoners were jealous of their captives cushy trips to camps in the United Kingdom. There were also reports of prisoners being robbed and then killed and I suspect that this occurred on both sides, although how common this was is impossible to say. In many cases, when prisoners did not make it from the frontline to the rear of the lines their death was blamed on shelling. Graves told of two examples he knew of. In one case a soldier put grenades with their pins taken out in the pockets of three prisoners and then jumped into cover as they exploded, while in another twelve German soldiers were ordered out of a dug out, robbed, and then sent back into the dugout and grenades thrown in after them. There were also numerous statements by German soldiers who said that they saw British soldiers being murdered after capture and I do not have any doubts that this did happen, although there were many rumours of atrocities; the one that told of two Canadian officers being crucified by German troops seemed to be known all over the battlefields and at home. When Morgan tried to prove this event for his book on German Atrocities he could find no one who saw it.

The treatment of alien civilian internees was a very different matter to that of the military prisoners. The internment of civilians during wartime was rare and before the war the only example of large scale civilian internment was that carried out by the British during the Boer War. An event that was to see the birth of concentration camps in which many civilians died and the British were criticised widely around the world. The internment of civilians in the First World War was begun by the British and it was only after this that Germany began to intern British civilians in Germany. The eventual internment of so many supposedly enemy aliens in the First World War is now seen as an over-reaction, but it was in part a response to the changing public mood, which was in part encouraged by the government. The outbreak of war did lead to a panic in Britain over enemy spies and saboteurs, which was encouraged by certain elements of the press. There were very few cases of violence by the public towards those seen as enemy aliens in the early days of the war, but this was to change.

Indeed, the British government had no plans to intern all aliens, not even those from enemy countries; it was a scheme that would have been fraught with difficulties on such a large scale. The internment of all enemy aliens was eventually instituted by pressure from the public and the severe violence against these peoples, many of whom were originally arrested for their own protection. It is often said that the large scale internment was forced on the government by the public, press, and pressure from right-wing politicians. However, much of the anti-German feeling of the time was incited by Government actions and by the powerful propaganda that they were employing. The founding of the Secret War Propaganda Bureau under Charles Masterman was a government idea, with the sole aim to encourage anti-German feeling using some of the best known writers of the time. Surely those responsible must have been aware of how successful this would be amongst the working classes who were easily influenced by what they read in the newspapers. Blaming sections of the press for this must be seen in the context of the period. There was some government control over how the war was reported in the press. This censorship could surely have been extended to stop some of the ridiculous stories about aliens living in this country that appeared in the national press, but these did seem to support the government aims of promoting anti-German feeling and were inspired by those writers working with Masterman.

The government then found themselves in a difficult position. They were promoting anti-German feeling, but not wanting to be seen to act in a similar way to the Germans by persecuting innocent civilians. The government did stand up to numerous calls for the reprisals against the German military prisoners held in this country after British prisoner's bad treatment in Germany; they claimed that such actions would not be the British way. The attempts early in the war to hold U-boat crews in less welcoming accommodation had also shown that any poor treatment would lead to retaliation by the Germans. There also seemed to be a different feeling amongst the public towards German soldiers held in Britain than there were against alien citizens. Despite the stories of atrocities towards the Belgian people early in the war, German soldiers were often presented with gifts by the public on their way to the camps. Later when other German atrocities became public knowledge it was German civilians that seemed to bear the greatest hatred of the public. Whatever the reasons for the eventual internment of the majority of enemy aliens there situation was very different from that of the German military prisoners. There was a difference in how civilian internees felt about their imprisonment and how military prisoners saw theirs. There is little doubt that many of the military prisoners found the camps preferable to the discomfort and horror of the trenches. Boredom was in most cases preferable to the danger of being blown to pieces, though there were some who wanted to get back and fight, but these were in the minority. On the whole, the civilian internees had a different view. They felt that a great wrong had been done to them—they had been imprisoned, but had committed no crime. The hatred they may have felt against those responsible may have also turned towards their fellow inmates who they could find no escape from.

The suffering of innocent men imprisoned for years was only one aspect of the problem that internment caused. Outside the camps there were many women who were thrown into poverty with their children because their husbands had been taken from them. Many of these were British citizens whose only crime was to meet and fall in love with a German. Many of the children who suffered because of internment were British born and had never known any other country. They had suddenly become enemies in their own country, shunned by their friends and forced to grow up without a father.

What was common to both military and civilian was the effort that it took to conform to the conventions of life. Many prisoners became depressed and found little will to do anything. There seemed no need to wash or shave or, in some cases, even dress. It was easy for the prisoners to let themselves go when time meant nothing and there is no aim or object, but it was important to make an effort. As Paul Cohen-Portheim put it, 'self-respect and the shaving brush live in mystical union'.

Whatever the reason for the imprisonment of large numbers of civilians during the war it is now seen as an unfair and in most cases unneeded action by the government. The British, however, were able to present a civilised and caring face to the world while portraying the Germans as savages. It may well have been the British use of internment for civilians that led to similar actions in other countries involved in the war. The reasons for internment and the fact that it was done at all were an overreaction, but once it was in force then I would argue that Britain did it as well, if not better, than the enemy.

To end I would like to include a quote from Morris Lamb. Mr Lamb worked for the Jewish Joint Distribution Committee, an American charity that operated in the Jewish internment camps in Cyprus after the Second World War, 'if I had to be incarcerated in a camp, I would choose the British to be my keepers'. I think that says it all.

Appendix:
Prisoner of War
and Internment Camps

This is by no means a complete list of the camps used in the First World War. There are no doubt many camps that have been missed from this list and for that I apologise, but the site of many of the smaller camps have been lost. The memory of these camps have long since passed with the people who would have known about them.

Abbess Roding	The Old rectory, Abbess Roding, Ongar Essex.
Abbey Dore	42 West St, Leominster, Herefordshire.
Abergavenny	The Garage, Abergavenny, Monmouthshire.
Aberglasney	Aberglasney, Carmarthan, South Wales.
Aber Llowyn House	Aber Llowyn House, Llanfarian, Cardiganshire.
Addington Park Hospital	Addington Park War Hospital, Croydon Surrey.
Addlestone	Addlestone, Surrey.
Aldborough	Aldborough, Norwich, Norfolk.
Aldershot Isolation Hospital	Isolation Hospital, Aldershot.
Alexandra Palace	Alexandra Palace, Wood Green, London.
Alton	Alton, Hampshire.
Ambergate	Crich Matlock, Ambergate, Derby.
Ampthill	Ampthill, Bedfordshire.

Arrington	Kardwick Arms, Arrington, Cambridgeshire.
Ashbourne	Ashbourne, Derbyshire.
Ashby-de-la-Zouch	Queens Head Hotel, Ashby-de-la-Zouch, Leicestershire.
Ashwell	Ashwell, Hertfordshire.
Atherstone	Atherstone, Warwickshire.
Axbridge	Axbridge, Somerset.
Badsey Manor	Badsey Manor, Badsey, Worcestershire.
Baldersby Park	Home farm, Baldersby Park, Yorkshire.
Baldock	Malting House, Baldock, Hertfordshire.
Banbury	Banbury, Oxfordshire.
Barnstone	Langor Hall, Barnstone, Nottinghamshire.
Beachley	Beachley, Chepstow, Monmouth.
Beaminster	Beaminster, Dorset.
Beauly	Beauly, Lentran, Inverness-shire.
Beckenham	Beckenham, Kent.
Bedford Military Hospital	Bedford Military Hospital, Bedfordshire.
Belmont House	Belmont House, Chigwell, Essex.
Berkhampstead	Berkhampstead, Hertforshire.
Berkswell	Berkswell, Hampton in Arden, Warwickshire.
Bethnal Green Military Hospital	Military Hospital, Cambridge Rd, Bethnal Green, London.
Billericay	Billericay, Essex.
Billingford	Billingford Maltings, near Diss, Norfolk.
Binegar	Binegar, Somerset.
Birmingham Hospital	1st Southern General Hospital, Edgbaston, Birmingham.
Bishop Stortford	Oak Hall, Bishops Stortford, Hertfordshire.
Blaisdon	Blaisdon Gloucestershire.
Blandford	Blandford, Dorset.
Bletchley	Watling St, Bletchley, Bucks.
Blunham	Blunham, Bedfordshire.
Boddam	Boddam, near Peterhead, Aberdeen.

Bolsover Castle	Bolsover Castle, Chesterfield.
Boroughbridge	Boroughbridge, West Riding, Yorkshire.
Boston Dock	Boston Dock, Lincolnshire.
Bovington	Bovington, Dorset.
Bracebridge	Bracebridge, Lincolnshire.
Brackley	Brackley, Northamptonshire.
Bradford Abbas	Bradford Abbas, near Yeovil, Somerset.
Brailes	Springfield House, Brailes, Warwickshire.
Braemore	Braemore, Loch Doon, Near Ullapool, Ross-shire.
Bramley	Bramley near Basingstoke, Hampshire.
Brampton	Brampton, Hampshire.
Braughing	Oak Hall, Bishop Stortford, Hertfordshire
Brecon	County Prison, Brecon, Wales.
Bretby Hall	Bretby Hall, Burton on Trent, Staffordshire.
Brighton General Hospital	2nd Eastern General Hospital, Brighton, Sussex.
Brightwell	Brightwell, Berkshire.
Brixworth	Brixworth, Northamptonshire.
Broad Marston	The Priory, Broad Marston, Warwickshire.
Brockenhurst	Brockenhurst, Hampshire.
Brocton Camp	P/W Camp, Brocton, Staffordshire.
Brocton Camp Hospital	P/W Hospital Brocton.
Bromfield	42 West St, Leominster, Herefordshire.
Bromyard	42 West St, Leominster, Herefordshire.
Bucknall	Tupholme Hall, Bucknall Bardney, Lincolnshire.
Bulford	Bulford, Wiltshire.
Buntingford	Hare St, Buntingford, Hertfordshire.
Burnham Market	Burnham Market, Norfolk.
Burton Hall	Burton Hall, Lincolnshire.
Burton upon Trent	Burton upon Trent, Staffordshire.
Buxton	Peak Dale, Buxton, Derby.

Caersws	Caersws, Montgomery.
Cambridge	Newmarket Road, Cambridge.
Cambridge Hospital	Cambridge Hospital, Aldershot.
Cambridge Military Hospital	Cambridge Military Hospital, Cambridge.
Caolasnacon	Caolasnacon, near Kinlochleven, Argyllshire.
Cardiff	3rd Western General Hospital, Cardiff.
Carlton	Carlton, Near Kelham, Nottinghamshire.
Carmarthen	Carmarthen, Wales.
Castle Bromwich	Castle Bromwich, near Birmingham.
Catterick	Catterick. Yorkshire.
Catterick Military Hospital	Military Hospital, Catterick.
Cawood	Fosters Flour Mills, Cawood, Selby, W Riding, Yorkshire.
Caxton	Caxton, Cambridgeshire.
Caythorpe	Caythorpe, Lincolnshire.
Chapel-en-le-Frith	Bank Hall, Chapel-en-le-Frith, Derbyshire.
Chapel Oak	Chapel Oak, Iron Cross, Salford Priors, Warwickshire.
Cheam	Cheam, Surrey.
Chelmsford	Chelmsford, Essex.
Chelsea Hospital	2nd London General Hospital, St Marks College, Chelsea, London.
Cheltenham	Cheltenham, Gloucester.
Cheriton Bishop	Cheriton Bishop, Devon.
Chesterton	Chesterton, Cambridgeshire.
Chevington	Chevington, Bury St Edmunds, Suffolk.
Chigwell	Foxbarrow Farm, Chigwell Rd, Essex.
Chippenham	Chippenham Wiltshire.
Chipping Norton	Chipping Norton, Oxfordshire.
Chipping Ongar	Chipping Ongar, Essex.
Chiseldon	Chiseldon Wiltshire.
Chiseldon Military Hospital	Chiseldon Wiltshire.
Cholsey	Cholsey, Devon.
Churchdown	Churchdown, Gloucestershire.
Churt	Churt, Farnham, Surrey.

Cilian Aeron	Cilian Aeron, Cardigan.
Cirencester	Cirencester, Gloucestershire.
City of London Military Hospital	42 Clifden Rd, Homerton.
Claydon	Claydon, Suffolk.
Clee Hill Dhu	Clee Hill Dhu, Shropshire.
Clent	Clent, Worcester.
Cleobury Mortimer	Cleobury Mortimer, Salop.
Codford	Codford Wiltshire.
Colchester Hospital	Military Hospital, Colchester, Essex.
College Town	College Town, Camberley, Surrey.
Colsterdale	Colsterdale, near Masham, Yorkshire.
Compton	Compton, Berkshire.
Coningsby	Coningsby, Lincolnshire.
Connaught Hospital	Connaught Hospital, Aldershot, Hampshire.
Conveth Mains	Conveth Mains, Laurencekirk, Kincardine.
Copt Hewick Hall	Copt Hewick Hall, near Ripon, Yorkshire.
Corby	Corby, near Kettering, Northamptonshire.
Corfton Hall	42 West St, Leominster, Herefordshire.
Cove	Farnborough, Hampshire.
Cranleigh	Cranleigh, Surrey.
Crawford	Crawford, Lanarkshire.
Crichel	Crichel, Blandford, Dorset.
Crickhowell	Crickhowell, South Wales.
Crondall	Crondall, Hampshire.
Crowthorne War Hospital	Crowthorne, Berkshire.
Croxton Park	Croxton Park, Melton Mowbray, Leicestershire.
Cuddington	Cuddington, Chesire.
Cumnor	Cumnor, Oxfordshire.
Dartford War Hospital	Dartford, Kent.
Dawyck	Dawyck, Stobo, Peebles.
Deal Royal Marine Infirmary	Deal, Kent.
Deddington	Deddington, Oxon.
Denby	Denby near Darby.

Denham Lodge	Denham Lodge, Uxbridge, Middlesex.
Devizes	Devizes, Wiltshire.
Devonport Hospital	Military Hospital, Devonport.
Digby	Digby, Lancashire.
Dolyhir	Dolyhir, Kingston, Herefordshire.
Donington Hall	Castle Donington, Derby.
Dorchester	Dorchester.
Dorking	Dorking, Surrey.
Douglas	Douglas, Isle of Man.
Dover Military Hospital	Dover, Kent.
Downham Hall	Brandon, Suffolk.
Drim Wood	Narbeth, Pembroke, South Wales.
Droitwich	Droitwich, Worcestershire.
Drumbuach	Drumbuach, Methven.
Dulverton	Dulverton, Somerset.
Dunmow	Dunmow, Essex.
Dykebar War Hospital	Dykebar. Paisley.
Eardiston	Eardiston, Tenbury Wells, Worcestershire.
Eartham	Slindon, near Chichester.
Easingwold	North Riding, Yorkshire.
Eastcote	Pinner, Middlesex.
East Dereham	East Dereham, Norfolk.
Eastgate	Rosehill Farm, Eastgate, County Durham.
East Grinstead	East Grinstead, Sussex.
East Leake	Loughborough, Leicestershire.
East Leeds War Hospital	Harehills Rd, Leeds.
Easton on the Hill	Near Stamford, Northamptonshire.
East Preston	Angmering, Sussex.
Edinburgh	The Detention House, Edinburgh Castle.
Edinburgh Castle Hospital	Castle Military Hospital, Edinburgh.
Eggesford	Eggesford, Devon.
Ellesmere	42 West St, Leominster, Herefordshire.
Elton	Elton, Hampshire.
Enfield	Clayhill Lodge, Enfield, Middlesex.

Epping	Epping, Essex.
Estuary Road	Estuary Road, King's Lynn, Norfolk.
Ettingshall	Bilston, Staffordshire.
Etwall	Etwall, Derby.
Evesham	Evesham, Worcestershire.
Eye	Eye, Suffolk.
Falmouth Military Hospital	Falmouth, Cornwall.
Fargo Rolleston Military Hospital	Salisbury, Wiltsshire.
Faringdon	Pidnall House, Faringdon, Berks.
Feltham	Feltham, Middlesex.
Fladbury	Craycombe House, Fladbury, Pershore, near Worcester.
Flowerdown	Flowerdown, Winchester, Hampshire.
Folkingham	Folkingham, Lincolnshire.
Forgandenny	Forgandenny, Perthshire.
Forteviot	Forteviot, Perthshire.
Fovant	Fovant, Wiltshire.
Frampton-on-Severn	Frampton-on-Severn, Gloucester.
Frith Hill	Headquarters, Blackdown, Surrey.
Frome	Keyford, Frome, Somerset.
Frongoch	Frongoch, near Bala, North Wales.
Fulham Military Hospital	St Dunstans Rd, Hammersmith, London.
Gaminlay	Sandy, Bedfordshire.
German Hospital	Dalston, London.
Gillingham	Gillingham, Dorset.
Gisburn	Gisburn, West Riding, Yorkshire.
Glasgow	3rd Scottish General Hospital, Glasgow.
Glasgow	4th Scottish General Hospital, Glasgow.
Glatton	Glatton, Huntingdonshire.
Glendevon	Glendevon, Dollar, Clackmannanshire.
Glentham	Glentham, Market Rasen, Lincolnshire.
Gore Farm	Dartford, Kent.
Grantham	Belton Park, Grantham, Lincolnshire.

Grays	The Wouldham Cement Company, Grays, Essex.
Great Baddow	Great Baddow, Essex.
Great Coggeshall	Great Coggeshall, Essex.
Great Hale	Great Hale, Heckington, Lincolshire.
Great Hampton	Great Hampton, Evesham, Worcestershire.
Great Offley	Great Offley, Hertfordshire.
Great Ouseburn	Great Ouseburn, Yorkshire.
Great Witley	Great Witley, Worcestershire.
Green Lane Farm	Near Doncaster, West Riding, Yorkshire.
Gringley-on-the-Hill	West Gainsborough, Lincolnshire.
Guilsborough	Guilsborough, Northamptonshire.
Hackney Wick	Gainsborough Road, London.
Hailsham	Hailsham, Sussex.
Halam	Southwell, Nottinghamshire.
Halesworth	Halesworth, Suffolk.
Hallatrow	Hallatrow, Somerset.
Halling	Lees Cement Works, Halling, Snodland, Kent.
Halstead	Halstead, Essex.
Halton Park	Wendover, Buckinghamshire.
Hammersmith Military Hospital	Duncane Rd, Shepherds Bush, London.
Handforth	Rubber Works, Handforth, Chesire.
Harewood	Harewood, West Riding, Yorkshire.
Harperley	Harperley Station, County Durham.
Hatfield	Hatfield, Hertfordshire.
Hatherleigh	Hatherleigh, Devon.
Hatherton	Hatherton, near Nantwich, Chesire.
Hatley St George	The Rectory, Hatley St George, Gamlingway, Sandy, Bedfordshire.
Haughley	Haughley, Suffolk.
Haughton Lodge	Market Harborough Leicestershire.
Haverfordwest	Haverfordwest, Pembroke.
Hawksbury	Hawksbury, Upton.
Haywards Heath	Haywards Heath, Sussex.
Heacham	Heacham, Norfolk.

Hemel Hempstead	Hemel Hempstead, Hertfordshire.
Henfield	Henfield, Sussex.
Hermitage	The Hermitage, Crickhowell, Brecon.
Heavingham	Saxmundham, Suffolk.
Hogsthorpe	Hogsthorpe, Lincolnshire.
Holbeach	Holbeach, Lincolnshire.
Hollowell	Hollowell Grange, Creaton, Northamptonshire.
Holyport	Holyport, near Bray, Maidenhead, Berkshire.
Honiton	Honiton, Devon.
Horsham	Horsham, Suffolk.
Houghton Regis	Houghton Regis, Bedfordshire.
Hove	Brooker Hall, Hove, Sussex.
Huntingdon	Huntingdon, Huntingdonshire.
Hunton Bridge	Kings Langley, Hertfordshire.
Hursley Park	Standon, Hursley, near Winchester, Hampshire.
Ilchester	Near Yeovil, Somerset.
Ilkeston	Oakwell Colliery Buildings, Ilkeston, Derby.
Illeston	Illeston Grange, Market Harborough, Leicestershire.
Inverlaidnan	Carr Bridge, Inverness-shire.
Ipswich Military Hospital	Ipswich, Suffolk.
Isleworth	Isleworth, Middlesex.
Islington	St Mary's Institute, Cornwallis Rd, Islington, London.
Itton	Cottage Farm, Itton, Chepstow, Monmouth.
Ivybridge	Lee Mill Ivybridge, Devon.
Iwerne Minster	near Blandford, Dorset.
Jersey	Jersey, Channel Islands.
Justinhaugh	Newmiln of Craigeassie, Justinhaugh.
Kedington	Near Haverhill, Suffolk.
Kegworth	Kegworth, Derby.
Kelham	Kelham Brickfields, Kelham, Newark, Nottinghamshire.

Kempshott Park	Kempshott House, Basingstoke, Hampshire.
Kenilworth	Kenilworth, Warwickshire.
Kenninghall	East Harling, Norfolk.
Kerry Newtown	Montgomeryshire.
Kettleburgh	Wickham Market, Suffolk.
Keyston	Keyston, Hampshire.
Kimbolton	The Stables, Kimbolton Castle, Kimbolton, Huntingdonshire.
King George Hospital	Stamford St, London.
King George V. Hospital	Dublin.
Kingsbridge	Kingsbridge, Devon.
Kingsbury	Kingsbury, Warickshire.
King's Lynn	St James Hall, King's Lynn, Norfolk.
Kinlochleven	Kinlochleven, Argyllshire.
Kinmel Park Military Hospital	Kinmel Park, Denbigh.
Kintello	Bridge of Earn, Perthshire.
Knockaloe	Knockaloe, Isle of Man.
Knutsford	Knutsford, Cheshire.
Ladbroke Hall	Harbury, Southam, Warwick.
Lakenham	Lakenham Mills, near Norwich, Norfolk.
Lambourne	Lambourne, Berkshire.
Lampeter	Lampeter, Cardigan.
Lancaster Castle	Lancaster Castle, Lancashire.
Lancing	Lancing, Sussex.
Laneham	Retford, Nottinghamshire.
Langley Park	Iver Heath, Buckinghamshire.
Langton Priory	Guildford, Surrey.
Larkhill	Salisbury Plain, Wiltshire.
Lawford Heath	Rugby, Warwickshire.
Leasowe	Leasowe Castle, near Birkenhead.
Ledbury	42 West St, Leominster, Herefordshire.
Leicester Hospital	No. 5 Northern General Hospital, Leicester.
Leigh	Leigh, Lancashire.
Leigh	Leigh, near Worcestershire.
Leighterton	Tetbury, Gloucestershire.
Leighton Buzzard	20 Market Square, Leighton Buzzard, Bedfordshire.
Leominster	Leominster, Herefordshire.

Lewes	North St, Lewes, Sussex.
Lewisham Military Hospital	Military Hospital, Lewisham, London.
Leystone Farm	Leystone Farm, Perthshire.
Libury Hall	Libury Hall, Ware, Hertfordshire.
Lincoln Hospital	4th Northern General Hospital, Lincolnshire.
Linton	Linton, Cambridgeshire.
Little Balbrogie	Little Balbrogie, Ardler.
Littleport	Near Ely, Cambridgeshire.
Liverpool Hospital	1st Western General Hospital, Fazakerley, Liverpool.
Llanafon	Grogwynion House, Llanafon, Near Aberystwyth.
Llanbedr	Penyalt Hall, Llanbedr, Merionethshire.
Llandebie	Lime Farm Buildings Llandebie, Carmarthen.
Llandinabo	42 West St, Leominster, Herefordshire.
Llanerchymedd	The Workhouse, Llanerchymedd, Anglesea.
Llanmartin	42 West St, Leominster, Herefordshire.
Long Ashton	Long Ashton, Bristol.
Long Clawson	The Hall, Long Clawson, Leicestershire.
Loughborough	The Workhouse, Loughborough, Leicestershire.
Machynlleth	Machynlleth, Montgomeryshire.
Magdalen Camp Military Hospital	Military Hospital, Magdalen Camp, Winchester, Hampshire.
Maldon	Maldon, Essex.
Manchester Hospital	Nell Lane, Military Hospital, West Didsbury, Manchester.
Marcham	Marcham, Berkshire.
Market Harborough	No. 2 Agricultural Depot, Market Harborough, Leicestershire.
Marks Tey	Marks Tey, Essex.
Marshmoor	Marshmoor Sidings, North Mimms, Hertfordshire.

Martlesham	Martlesham Heath, Woodbridge, Suffolk.
Martley	Mayland, Maldon, Essex.
Melchbourne	Melchbourne, Bedfordshire.
Meldreth	Near Royston, Cambridgeshire.
Midhurst	Midhurst, Sussex.
Mildenhall	Mildenhall, Suffolk.
Mile End Military Hospital	Bancroft Road, London.
Millbank Hospital	Queen Alexandria Hospital, Grosvenor Rd, London.
Milldown	Dorchester, Dorset.
Mill Hill	Mill Hill, Middlesex.
Milnthorpe	Milnthorpe, Westmoreland.
Monkspath	Monkspath, Warwickshire.
Morton	Morton, Lincolnshire.
Mundford	West Tofts, Mundford, Norfolk.
Napsbury War Hospital	St Albans.
Narborough	The Workhouse, Narborough, Leicestershire.
Netheravon Aerodrome	The Aerodrome, Netheravon, Wiltshire.
Netley Hospital	Royal Victoria Hospital, Netley.
Newcastle Hospital	1st Northern General Hospital, Newcastle.
Newlandside	Stanhope, County Durham.
Newport Hospital	3rd Western General Hospital, Newport.
Newport Pagnall	Headquarters, Westbury House, Newport Pagnell, Buckinghamshire.
Newton Abbot	The Institute, Newton Abbot, Devon.
Nocton	Nocton, Lincolnshire.
Normanton	Stamford, Lincolnshire.
Normanton Hall	The Workhouse, Loughborough, Leicestershire.
Northallerton	East Riding, Yorkshire.
Northfield	Northfield, Worcestershire.
North Kilworth	The Hawthorns, North Kilworth, Leicestershire.
North Leach	Gloucestershire.
North Lew	Devon.
Northolt	The Neddles, Northolt, Middlesex.

North Ripon	No. 8, North Camp, Ripon, Yorkshire.
Norton Barracks Military Hospital	Norton Barracks, Worcestershire.
Norton Cukney	Mansfield, Nottinghamshire.
Okendon	South Okendon, Romford, Essex.
Offchurch Bury	Offchurch Bury, Warwickshire.
Orfordness	Orfordness, Suffolk.
Oswestry	Eastern Camp, Park Hall, Oswestry, Salop.
Oswestry (officers)	Camp Park Hall, Oswestry, Salop.
Oswestry P/W Hospital	Park Hall Camp, Oswestry, Salop.
Oswestry	Western Camp, Park Hall, Oswestry, Salop.
Otley	West Riding, Yorkshire.
Oundle	Oundle, Northamptonshire.
Oxted	Oxted, Surrey.
Panshanger	Panshanger, Hertfordshire.
Papplewick	Papplewick, Nottinghamshire.
Partney	Partney, Lincolnshire.
Pateley Bridge	West Riding, Yorkshire.
Pattishall	Near Towcester, Northamptonshire.
Peasmarsh	Rye, Sussex.
Penarth	Glamorgan, South Wales.
Penmaenmawr	Penaenmawr, Carnavon.
Penshurst	Penshurst, Kent.
Peopleton	Pershore, Worcestershire.
Penham Down	Salisbury Plain, Wiltshire.
Pershore	Pershore, Worcestershire.
Pinchbeck Road	Spalding, Lincolnshire.
Plumtree	Plumtree Nottinghamshire.
Podington	Near Wellingborough, Northamptonshire.
Port Clarence	Middlesbrough, Yorkshire.
Port Talbot	Port Talbot, Glamorgan.
Portsmouth Hospital	5th Southern General Hospital, Poertsmouth.
Potters Bar	Potters Bar, Middlesex.

Potton	Potton, Bedfordshire.
Purfleet Military Hospital	Military Hospital, Purfleet.
P/W Hospital Belmont	Belmont, near Sutton, Surrey.
P/W Hospital Brocton	Brocton Camp, Staffordshire.
Raasay	Raasay, Kyle.
Radford	Near Coventry, Warwickshire.
Ragdale Hall	Ragdale Hall, Leicestershire.
Rainham	Rainham, Essex.
Ramsbury	Barney Farm, Ramsbury, Wiltshire.
Ranskill	The Maltings, Ranskill, Nottinghamshire.
Reading War Hospital	War Hospital, Reading, Berkshire.
Redhill	Redhill, Surrey.
Redmires	Sheffield, Yorkshire.
Retford	Retford, Nottinghamshire.
Rhoose	Kemey's Hotel, Rhoose, near Cardiff.
Richmond Military Hospital	Grove Road, Richmond, Surrey.
Rickmansworth	Rickmansworth, Hertfordshire.
Riding Mill	Slaley PO, Riding Mill, Northumberland.
Rippingale Fen	Rippingale, Lincolnshire.
Robertsbridge	Robertsbridge, Sussex.
Rochford	Rochford, Essex.
Rockland All Saints	Rockland, Attleborough, Norfolk.
Romsey	Romsey, Hampshire.
Ross-on-Wye	Ross-on-Wye, Herefordshire.
Roysth	Inverkeiting, Rosyth, Fifeshire.
Rothwell	Kettering, Northamptonshire.
Rowley	Healeyfield, Castleside, near Consett, County Durham.
Rowrah	Rowrah, Cumberland.
Rumshott	Rumshott Wood, Sevenoaks, Kent.
Rushden	Rushden House, Rushden, Northamptonshire.
Ruthin	Bathafarm Hall, Ruthin, Denbighshire.
Ruthwell	Ironhurst, Ruthwell, Dunfries.

Saffron Wadon	The Union, Saffron Wadon, Essex.
St Albans	St Albans, Hertfordshire.
Saltram	Saltram, Woodford, Plympton, Devon.
Sandgate	Storrington, Sussex.
Sandhill Park	Near Taunton, Somerset.
Sawley	Sawley, Yorkshire.
Semer	Haughley, Suffolk.
Send	Boughton Hall, Send, Surrey.
Sheffield Hospital	3rd Northern General Hospital, Sheffield.
Shelsley Walsh	Shelsley Walsh, Worcestershire.
Shepton Mallet	Shepton Mallet, Somerset.
Shere	Holmbury St Mary, Shere, Surrey.
Shirehampton	Shirehampton, near Bristol.
Shotley	Naval Sick Quarters, Shotley, Harwich.
Shotley	H M Training Establishment, Shotley, Harwich.
Shouldham	Shouldham, Norfolk.
Shrewsbury	Abbey Wood, Shrewsbury.
Sidbury	Sidbury, Devon.
Sinnington	North Riding, Yorkshire.
Skipton Officers Camp	Skipton, Yorkshire.
Sleaford	The Union, Sleaford, Lincolnshire.
Slough	Slough, Buckinghamshire.
Soberton	Soberton, Hampshire.
Soho Pool	Soho Pool, near Birmingham.
Somerby Hall	Gainsborough, Lincolnshire.
Somerford Hall	Breewood, Staffordshire.
Southampton	Skating Rink Receiving Depot, Bevois Mount, Southampton.
South Brent	Coranation Hall, South Brent, Devon.
South Cleatham	South Cleatham, Middlesborough.
Southill Park	Southill Park, Bedfordshire.
South Molton	South Molton, Devon.
Spalding	The Union, Spalding, Lincolnshire.
Stainby	Grantham, Lincolnshire.
Stainton Sidings	Dalton-in-Furness.
Stanford Le Hope	Stanford le Hope, Essex.

Stanley Moor	Ladmanlow, Burbage, Buxton.
Stanstead	Oak Hall, Bishops Stortford, Hertfordshire.
Starcross	Starcross, Devon.
Steeple Bumpstead	near Haverhill, Sussex.
Steyning	Steyning, Sussex.
Stobs	Hawick, Scotland.
Stobs P/W Hospital	P/W Hospital, Stobs, Hawick, Scotland.
Stoke Edith	42 West St, Leominster, Herefordshire.
Stoke Green	Stoke Green, Buckinghamshire.
Stone	Stone Staffordshire.
Stoulton	Whittington, Worcestershire.
Stowell	Stowell, Somerset.
Stow Park	Stow Park, Lincolnshire.
Stratford-upon-Avon	Shotterby, Stratford-upon-Avon.
Sudbury	Sudbury, Derbyshire.
Sutton Veny	Sutton Veny, Wiltshire.
Swanage	Swanage, Dorset.
Tadcaster	The Workhouse, Tadcaster, West Riding, Yorkshire.
Talgarth	Fregunter Park, Talgarth, Brecknock.
Taplow Canadian Hospital	Canadian Hospital, Taplow.
Tarrylaw	Tarrylaw Farm, near Balbeggie, Perthshire.
Taunton (officers)	Sandhill Park, Taunton.
Tempsford,	Bedfordshire.
Tendring	Tendring, Essex.
Tenterden	Tenterden, Kent.
Thing Hall	42 West St, Leominster, Herefordshire.
Thirsk	North Riding, Yorkshire.
Thornbury	Thornbury, Gloucestershire.
Thorpe Norfolk War Hospital	Norfolk War Hospital, Thorpe, Norfolk.
Thorp Satchville	Near Melton Mowbray, Leicestershire.
Timberland	The Maltings, Timberland, Lincolnshire.
Tiverton	Tiverton, Devon.
Tockwith	Near York, Yorkshire.

Toddington	Winchcombe, Gloucestershire.
Tooting Military Hospital	Church Lane, Tooting, London.
Tovil	Tovil, Kent.
Towyn	Neptune Hall, Towyn, Merionethshire.
Trawsfynydd	Trawsfynydd, Merioneth.
Turvey	Turvey, Bedfordshire.
Tutnall and Cobley	Tutnall, Bromsgrove, Worcestershire.
Tuxford	Tuxford, Nottinghamshire.
Twyford	Know Hill, Twyford, Berkshire.
Uckfield	Uckfield. Sussex.
Upavon	Upavon, Wiltshire.
Uppingham	Uppingham, Rutland.
Upton	The Vicarage, Upton, Northamptonshire.
Upton –on- Severn	Upton on Severn, Worcestershire.
Upware	Upware, Wicken, Cambridgeshire.
Usk	42 West St, Leominster, Herefordshire.
Uttoxeter	Uttoxeter, Staffordshire.
Waddesdon	Waddesdon, Buckinghamshire.
Wainfleet	Wainfleet, Lincolnshire.
Wakefield Officers Camp	Lofthouse Park, Wakefield.
Wakerley	Wakerley, Stamford, Northamptonshire.
Walsham le Willows	Walsham le Willows, Suffolk.
Wandsworth Hospital	3rd London General Hospital, Wandsworth, London.
Wantage	Wantage, Berkshire.
Warmsworth Hall	Warmsworth Hall, Doncaster.
Warren Wood	Croxton, Thetford, Norfolk.
Water Lane	Stratford, London
Watlington	Brightwell, Oxfordshire.
Wellesbourne	Holly Lodge, Wellesbourne, Warwickshire.
Welshpool	The Horse repository, Welshpool, Montgomery.
Wem	42 West St, Leominster, Herefordshire.
Weobly	42 West St, Leominster, Herefordshire.

West Ham	Abbey Mills, Manor Rd, West Ham, London.
West Mersea	West Mersea, Colchester, Essex.
Weston on the Green	Near Bicester, Oxfordshire.
Wetherby	The Brewery, Wetherby, West Riding, Yorkshire.
Whitewell	Whitewell, Norfolk.
Wigmore	Wigmore, Herefordshire.
Wilby	Wilby, Suffolk.
Willington	Willington Staffordshire.
Wimbourne	Wimbourne, Dorset.
Winchcomb	Winchcomb, Gloucestershire.
Wingland	Sutton Bridge, Wisbech, Lincolnshire.
Winwich	Winwich, Northamptonshire.
Wisborough Green	Wisborough Green, Sussex.
Withern	Near Alford, Lincolnshire.
Witney	Witney, Oxfordshire.
Woburn	Woburn, Bedfordshire.
Woking Detention Barracks	Detention Barracks, Woking.
Womenswold	Womenswold, Canterbury, Kent.
Woodborough	Woodborough, Nottinghamshire.
Woodham Ferrers	Woodham Lodge, Woodham Ferrers, Bicknacre, Essex.
Woodstock	Drill Hall, Woodstock, Oxon.
Wookey	Wookey, Somerset.
Woolwich Hospital	Royal Herbert Hospital, Woolwich, London.
Wootton Bassett	Corner House, Wootten Bassett, Wiltshire.
Worthy Down	Worthy Down, Winchester, Hampshire.
Wrotham	Bayldon House, Kingsdown, Wrothan, Sevenoaks, Kent.
Wrottesley	Wrottesley Hall, near Coolsall, Staffordshire.
Wymondham	Wymondham, Leicestershire.
Yardley Gobion	Stony Stratford, Buckinghamshire.
Yatesbury	Calne, Wiltshire.

Bibliography

Books

Bilton, D., *The Home Front in the Great War* (Pen & Sword, 2014)

Bloch, H., and Hill, G., *Germans in London* (All Points East)

Braithwaite, A., 'Emergency Committee for the Assistance of Germans, Austrians and Hungarians in Distress', *St Stephen's House, Friends Emergency Work in England 1914-1920*

Chapple, C., *Island of Barbed Wire* (Robert Hale, 2005)

Cohen-Portheim, P., *Time Stood Still* (Dutton, 1932)

Dove, R., ed., *'Totally un-English'?: Britain's Internment of Enemy Aliens in Two World Wars* (University of London, 2005)

Durnford, H., *Tunnelling to Freedom* (Dover, 2004)

Graves, R., *Goodbye to All That* (Penguin, 1957)

Harris, J., *Alexandra Palace, A Hidden History* (Tempus, 2005)

Morgan, J. H., *German Atrocities, An Official Investigation* (T. Fisher Unwin Ltd, 1916)

Morton, J., *Spies of the First World War* (National Archives, 2010)

Rippon, A., *Gunter Plüschow: Airman, Escaper and Explorer* (Pen & Sword, 2009)

Panayi, P., ed., *Germans in Britain Since 1500* (Hambeldon Press, 1996)

Rocker, R., *The London Years* (Robert Anscombe & Co Ltd, 1956)

Sargeaunt, B. E., *The Isle of Man and the Great War* (Douglas Brown & Sons, 1920)

Van Emden, R., and Humphries, S., *All Quiet on the Home Front* (Headline Books, 2003)

Van Emden, R., *Meeting the Enemy* (Bloomsbury, 2013)

Vischer, Dr A. L., *Barbed Wire Disease* (John Bale, Sons and Danielson, 1919)

Yarnall, J., *Barbed Wire Disease* (Spellmount, 2007)

Periodicals

'The European War', *New York Times Current History*, 1914–1920 (New York)

The Great War: I Was There, (Amalgamated Press Ltd: London)

The Illustrated War News

The Manchester Guardian

The Times

War Illustrated Album de Luxe (Amalgamated Press Ltd: London)

National Archive Documents

CAB/24/5

CAB/24/148/15

CAB/24/43

CAB/23/14

CAB/24/148/16

CAB/24/47

CAB/23/1

CAB/24/19

CAB/24/150